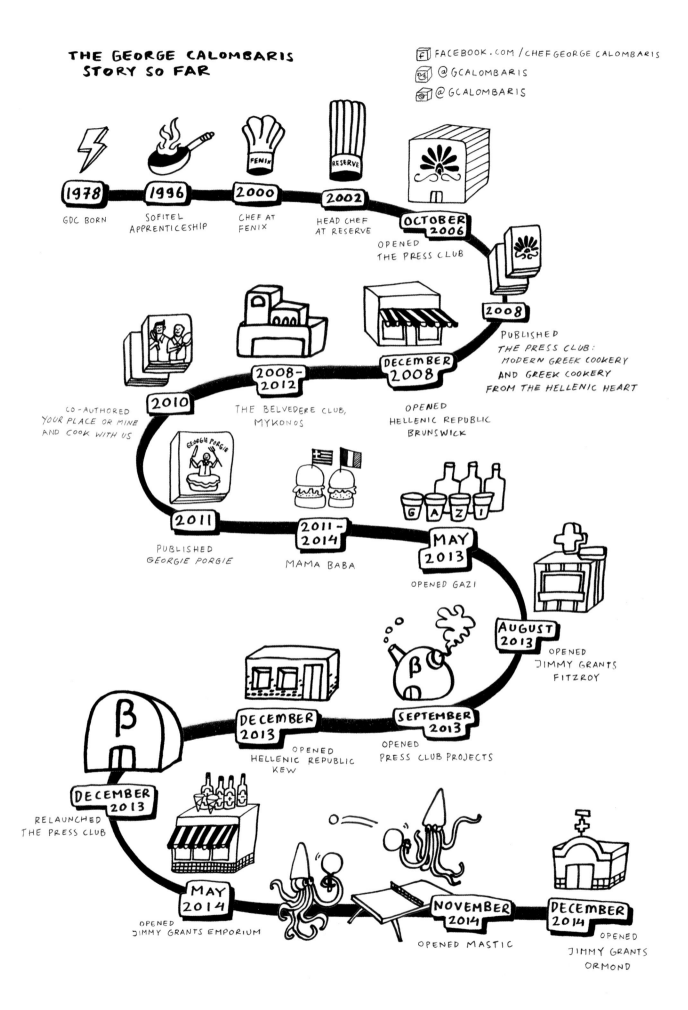

I dedicate this book to
the three most precious gifts
in my life : Natalie,
James and Michaela.
I am grateful
and thankful

GREEK

GEORGE CALOMBARIS

photography by *Earl Carter*

LANTERN

an imprint of
PENGUIN BOOKS

WHAT CAN I SAY?
ALL THE PEOPLE BELOW
HAVE PLAYED A HUGE PART
IN MY LIFE AND MEAN
THE WORLD TO ME. I THANK
THEM FOR THEIR SUPPORT
AND FRIENDSHIP, AND
AM HUMBLED BY THEIR
BEAUTIFUL WORDS ...

MARCO PIERRE WHITE
CHEF AND RESTAURATEUR, UK

Every major city in the world has great restaurants because they attract the talent and they can charge the price. I really like George's restaurant, Gazi. He's one of the cleverest chefs in Australia.

GREG MALOUF
CHEF AND RESTAURATEUR, RESTAURANT CLE, DUBAI

I love that George is as nuts about his Greek heritage as I am about my Lebanese one ... and we're always ribbing each other about which food is better! More importantly, he's a real 'everyman', he's always got time for people and he's a generous and loyal friend. Plus, he inspired me to lose 20 kg – you can't ask for more than that from a mate!

GARY MEHIGAN
CHEF AND MASTERCHEF AUSTRALIA JUDGE

How this man has grown in the last 10 years; he's unstoppable, inspirational and tireless. I don't know where he gets his energy from. As a chef, I admire how he thinks about food. He is, as everyone knows, creative, innovative and obsessive, but what I love about him is his cheeky sense of humour, his genuine good nature, his confidence and generosity of spirit. He is a great chef, a remarkable restaurateur, a good man and ... a good friend.

MATT PRESTON
FOOD WRITER AND MASTERCHEF AUSTRALIA JUDGE

THINGS I LOVE ABOUT GEORGE
He is all heart. He plates better than anyone I know. He dreams in flavours. He wears his heart on his sleeve. His blood runs blue with a love of the Victory. He can sleep ANYWHERE (which must help with the dreaming). He's so passionate about what he does and he still feels things deeply. He misbehaves. He's a good friend and (usually) a voice of reason – apart from the times when he's the voice of unreason, which is often when he's at his funniest. He also loves a negroni. He can be very, very silly. He doesn't talk about himself in the third person anymore. He's fun to tease about being a 'TV celebrity chef'.

THINGS I DON'T LOVE ABOUT GEORGE
His blood runs blue with a love of Carlton. He's a Man Utd fan. His trifle. His bottom often misbehaves. Umm, that's about it.

STELIOS PARLIAROS
PASTRY CHEF, SWEET ALCHEMY, GREECE

Good friend, worthy professional, loving father, a man with a deep understanding of others and a great sense of humour. These are the key features of George that make him so unique.

MICHALIS XATSIGIANNIS
MUSICAL ARTIST, GREECE

I met George a few years ago when I was in Australia doing concerts. From the very first moment I could see in his eyes a lively personality, full of energy, creativity and versatility. He is a really nice and sweet person who 'touches' you right away and makes you feel that he is really close to you.

His nostalgia for Greece has led him to the discovery of tastes that take you back to our bright and sunny country. One of his great advantages is to locate the needs and wishes of the people and to turn them into pleasures of taste. This is why he is so much accepted and appreciated. I hope that in the future we do have the possibility to combine his 'cultural' ability in cooking with my 'cooking' of music.

PETER ECONOMIDES
BRAND STRATEGIST, GREECE

George has a profound respect for his Greek DNA. Listen to these words from an introduction he gave to a dinner at The Press Club last year:

'Most people, when they think of Greek food, think of gyros and retsina. Not that there's anything wrong with gyros and retsina, but I'm going to show you there's a lot more to it than that.'

George, I love you. You know where you come from. And you know where you're going. GINETAI!

TRAVIS McAULEY
HEAD CHEF, HELLENIC REPUBLIC, MELBOURNE

George and I met back in 2006 prior to the opening of The Press Club and prior to MasterChef Australia. George has been my head chef, my business partner, my source of inspiration and, most of all, a good mate for the last 10 years.

We've cooked and demonstrated all over the country, and in fact the world – it's been incredible.

We've written and photographed hundreds of recipes together, for our own books, magazines and websites. In addition, we opened up The Press Club, Hellenic Republic Brunswick, Hellenic Republic Kew, Jimmy Grants and Mastic together, with a few more on the horizon.

The past 10 years have been a journey, a very busy journey, but certainly a fun one. All these experiences have given me long-lasting memories that I will always cherish.

ANTONIO CARLUCCIO
ITALIAN CHEF AND RESTAURATEUR, UK

I like the balance of George – not too many words but a lot of good deeds. Extremely ambitious, wanting to re-establish the legendary supremacy of the old Greek culture with panache. He can always crack a joke and appreciates good friendship.

ANTHEA GUERRA
GEORGE'S NIECE, MELBOURNE

My uncle George is someone that I look up to and someone who is always there for me.

He pours passion, effort and a load of determination into everything he does.

My uncle George inspires me to always follow my dreams and never give up.

CLAUDE BOSI
CHEF AND RESTAURATEUR, HIBISCUS, UK

George Calombaris? Size of a garden gnome – heart of a green giant. Got lots of time and love for that guy!

CHRISTO PESKIAS
CHEF AND RESTAURATEUR, P BOX, GREECE

George has the curiosity of a small child and the soul of a teenager. He always feels the need to 'play' which is, in my opinion, typical of great artists. But above all, he has an unbelievable sense of humour and although I see him once a year (I would like to see him more) I feel he is my soul mate.

SAT BAINS

CHEF AND RESTAURATEUR,
RESTAURANT SAT BAINS WITH ROOMS, UK

George; Georgie; Georgie Porgie; Georgiou; Mini me; Morph; Little one; Jr; Sat Jr; Knobber; Friend; Chef; Chief; Amazing guy; Legend. Oh and did I say Little one ...? Ha ha ha.

I jest of course; these are a few of the names I call George with great fondness. I've known George for several years now, and am privileged to say he's one of my true friends. I first met him in Melbourne when I was shopping – I saw a toddler with a beard in Baby Gap and realised it was George shopping for new clobber for his then recently appointed MasterChef gig. He does look rather dapper these days, I must admit.

Now on a serious note, I've been very lucky to know one of the most honest, humble and generous guys I've met in many years. We've had great times together, and share a passion for cooking, eating and sharing food around the table, which all equates to our incredible industry, hospitality.

I've seen first hand the way George works with and inspires his incredible teams at his restaurants, all very diverse in offering but all staying true to his Greek roots of looking after people once they walk through his door.

I've seen him nurture his team of loyal and dedicated staff and give them great opportunities as the company grows.

George's persona on MasterChef is of a true professional, wanting the guys to do well and getting almost as upset as them when they mess up, as he's a believer in these sometimes underdogs and wants them to make the most of the opportunity they have been given.

Then there's his food. I can honestly say that everything of George's that I've eaten has been utterly delicious. He's a cook's cook – his flavours are deep, honest and true, which comes from really understanding your ingredients as a true craftsman.

He's also embraced the importance of evolution by designating a development/test kitchen at Press Club Projects, allowing him and his team to explore trends and modern techniques to stay ahead of the pack.

Always looking, always learning, always pushing, never stopping, and constantly driving forward.

When I was asked to write a few words for this eagerly awaited and overdue cookbook, I was very honoured and privileged.

Thank you George.

Love you Chief.

HESTON BLUMENTHAL

CHEF AND RESTAURATEUR,
THE FAT DUCK, UK

Georgie Porgie pudding and pie, tried to kiss the girls but couldn't find a box big enough, so he cried, but I tell you what, puddings and pies he certainly can make!

He is fondly referred to as Georgie Demi Glaze Roussos by his two friends, and I feel proud and lucky to be counted as one of them (which makes Sat the only other friend he has).

George and I have some similarities, notably our lack of hair. Mine, however, is by choice, and George, by genetic diversion, has no choice: it's growing from his neck down.

This banter says a lot about George and the massive respect and admiration he's earned, not only in the industry but from the general public. He works unbelievably hard, is a truly inspiring chef, a great restaurateur, a motivator, mentor and above all, an incredible human being.

His role on MasterChef Australia has been a key catalyst for the biggest food explosion I have ever seen in a country, Australia. And that is because he truly cares. Truly cares about his craft, the contestants and human beings.

Like Sat, I too am truly honoured that George has given me the opportunity to pay homage to this bite-sized giant of the industry.

'Forever and ever and ever and ever, you'll be the one' Georgie.

RAYMOND CAPALDI
CHEF AND RESTAURATEUR, MELBOURNE

The culinary world is a chameleon of a job.

It can throw you around like a hurricane but when the calm sets in, you're ready to throw yourself back in there and take some more of the good, the bad and the ugly.

Don't get me wrong, this is a normal day for us chefs. We seem to become reliant on it, kind of an addiction really, that we seem to think we need in our lives.

In the late nineties, I arrived on the shores of Australia after a stint in Hong Kong. I had already been to Melbourne before, and wanted to come back. I loved the food culture and still rate this city as the best gastronomic place in the world, without the hype of London and New York. I was also drawn to a great sense of amity amongst its chefs, always willing to help each other, something which is still strong today.

I had taken my first Executive Head Chef position at The Regent Hotel (now Sofitel Melbourne on Collins). This was a huge challenge for me, being responsible for 90 chefs and six outlets servicing 1000 people at just 26 years of age. Furthermore, it was an establishment that had been resting on its past, the last bastion of the big kitchen brigade.

To achieve the standard of a three-hatted restaurant, which Sofitel's Le Restaurant later became, we needed to build a kitchen team full of passionate individuals. It may not have been a team where everybody got on, but they definitely wanted to be a part of it. The Regent was an incredibly food-focused hotel back then, quickly becoming the training ground for chefs as they learned all the foundations in every section of a kitchen.

To recruit apprentices, I started a programme which involved an interview and breakfast. The breakfast was to encourage candidates to come along with their parents so that I could get some real insights on them. It would be usual to have 25 candidates compete for nine apprentice chef positions.

It was during one of these breakfasts that my eyes were drawn to a young European-looking man who appeared very well dressed in a suit. Accompanied by his parents, it was not hard to see that he was very nervous.

When we finally got down to this nervous young man's interview and started to chat, there was this confidence without the arrogance. It was not hard to see that this young man was full of drive and determination and showed a willingness to learn. In my mind, I knew he was going to survive with the lions.

At the end of it, a lady (who happened to be his mother) approached me and said, 'If my son gets the job and you don't think he is pulling his weight, just give him a slap', but she guaranteed that this would never happen. She told me he was working in the family business before and after school and was a very hard-working young man.

This young man was George Calombaris.

George became part of the team at the Regent which happened to be one of the strongest and most inspirational teams I have ever worked with. If one of the chefs fell behind, there was always another to pick them up.

Even as a young apprentice, George gained great respect from the other chefs in the way he would quietly get on with his day-to-day work even when things were tough, soaking up as much knowledge up as he could, while always being very considerate to everyone in the kitchen.

After his apprenticeship George joined me and my co-partner Gary (Mehigan) as Head Chef at our restaurant Fenix in Richmond, where he continued to grow into the great success he is today.

Then there is the personal side. George has become one of my closest friends and I have the utmost respect for him. I've enjoyed many meals at his family's home and many soccer games with George's father, Demitri.

To me, George is the benchmark for any young dedicated chef. As someone who has trained his fair share of outstanding chefs, when you see dedication in a young man like I saw in George, you make sure you nurture it. I don't think I have ever pushed a chef so hard. There was something special about this young lad and I knew that I had to keep feeding him with as much knowledge as I could.

George and others like him have been the fuel to drive myself harder, to bring out the best in them, to bring out their unique underlying talent. It is for this reason that I continue to turn up every day and push them in this chameleon job as a chef.

I feel proud to be a part of George's journey so far, proud that he has continued to shape the Melbourne culinary landscape, and very proud that he continues to drive the masses of aspiring and developing chefs with very same qualities that I first recognised in him.

I look forward to seeing the rest of the story unfold, no doubt with many more exciting times ahead.

Contents

An Aussie chef with a Hellenic heart

I love listening to Greek music. It evokes an emotion in me like nothing else can, a feeling that I can't really put into words. Music draws me into the heart of Greece and gives me a sense of pride and belonging.

Food does the same thing. Traditional recipes tell the stories of those who went before us and bring us together in the spirit of generosity and love. And I'm so grateful that I grew up in a family that takes such pleasure from cooking for the people they love.

Of course I'm not a traditional cook. Far from it. People say to me 'oh, you're that Greek chef' but I'm not. I'm an Aussie and I cook Australian food. That's a can of worms right there: what is Australian food? Really, it's an amalgamation of all the food traditions that came to this country with the families who settled here. But because we're a young country and not locked into long-standing food traditions of our own we are able to play with it a bit, blur the lines and see what happens.

This is my kind of cooking. While I respect the recipes that have been handed down over the generations, I love to break the mould. Take Greek salad: yes, it should taste like Greek salad, with the fruity extra virgin olive oil, salty feta, ripe tomatoes, but why can't we push it in another direction? There's no reason why not, if you still respect where it came from.

And that's what this book is all about. It's a snapshot of my mind and my heart, the people and the memories that have influenced me and the food they have inspired me to create.

I was born to a Greek Cypriot mother and an Egyptian father (who had an Italian mother and a Greek father), so food at home was always interesting. One day it would be baked eggplant with mince, the next macaroni with fresh ricotta, and the next falafel with hummus. This was just normal for me, maybe even a bit embarrassing as my school friends often thought my food was weird. It was only later that I would truly appreciate what I was inheriting.

My mother was 12 when she came to Australia. She arrived with her mother and sisters and little else, apart from a big case half-filled with cooking equipment. My grandmother told me the people at customs didn't know what on earth a mortar and pestle was – they thought it must be some sort of weapon so they confiscated it! My mum had to work straight away – there was no choice as the family needed the money, so she spent many years working as a seamstress.

My dad didn't endure the struggles my mum and her family did. He was a much-loved only child, and grew up in an environment that valued tradition above all else. The family names on his side of the family have been passed down from generation to generation – I have them, my son has them and perhaps one day my grandson will too.

It's funny, I didn't learn to cook from my mother or grandmother. In fact, as kids we weren't allowed in the kitchen! What I did inherit from them was 'filotimo', a word that only exists in the Greek language and literally means to honour your friend. It is not something that can be taught – it means being born with an intrinsic sense of affection, generosity and hospitality.

I have a clear memory of one Easter, when I was about 10 years old. Following tradition, my dad came home with a whole lamb and put it in our bathtub, which was lined with black plastic. The lamb was coated in olive oil, garlic, onion, oregano and lemon and left to marinate overnight. The next day we got up early and got the fire going, while father and son prepared the lamb for the spit. He poured olive oil into my cupped hands and told me to rub it all over the lamb. I can still feel the oil in my hands to this day. It's moments like this that stay with us all our lives – a physical connection between the generations, and it's what I want to have with my kids too.

By the age of 14 I decided I wanted to be a chef. Either that or a soccer player, but it turns out I'm not very good at that! My dad wanted me to finish school so I worked part time at a local pasta restaurant, washing the dishes and absorbing whatever knowledge I could. As soon as I left school I got an apprenticeship, which was the best and toughest thing I've ever done. I came in at the end of the old-school era, where the kitchens were very noisy places – lots of yelling and screaming. I learnt a lot, and quickly. It worked for me as I can take that sort of pressure, but I wouldn't tolerate that sort of behaviour in my own kitchens, which are quieter and more respectful.

During those years I was devoted to the stovetop – nothing else mattered. I'm slightly ashamed to admit I didn't want a bar of Greek food then, preferring to work in a modern French restaurant. It was only when I became a head chef that I discovered a deep-seated love for Greek food. I knew instinctively that this was ME as a chef and belatedly grew to appreciate how lucky I was to have been given such a powerful inheritance. I cringe at my early ignorance now, but at least I got there in the end!

I visit Greece a couple of times a year, looking for 'something' – I never know what it is until I find it. Just sitting in an ancient city like Athens, sipping an ouzo and devouring a freshly made souvlaki really inspires me. The energy of the people gives me a total recharge, and I come back to Australia full of enthusiasm about what I'm going to cook next.

The idea behind The Press Club was to open a restaurant that non-Greeks would love to come to. And of course any Greeks would be a bonus too! I wanted to show people what modern Greek food was all about, steering well clear of the lamb souvlaki stereotypes.

(For the record, Greeks do not eat lamb all year round – we eat it at Easter. The rest of the time it's mainly pork or goat.)

My restaurants have always been a reflection of my past, my present and my future, but as any good restaurateur knows, you have to listen to what your customers want. Eventually I closed The Press Club to open Gazi, which is all about Greek street food – in short, the stuff I want to eat everyday. Food that has meaning and substance. The new Press Club has opened with a new dream, with my heart in the sun and my feet firmly in the kitchen.

Here, I offer my interpretion of modern Greek cooking, created by a proud Aussie with a Hellenic heart. The food has to be yummy, first and foremost, but it also has to be accessible and might occasionally nudge the cook to take that extra step, to be brave and try new things.

Through the food, the stories and the people who have influenced me this book represents who I am today. I want people to feel a sense of warmth when they look at the book or cook from it, and understand my beliefs in life. Not everything we do is successful, and it's okay to make mistakes. It's going to be fine! This should resonate in the recipes you cook and you should take confidence from that.

Just one word of advice: if you're not in the mood to cook, if you're just not feeling it, don't do it. Just read the book and enjoy the pictures, then come back when you're ready.

Most of all, I want this book to be something my kids will take off the shelf, read and perhaps cook from, and feel proud of their dad.

Filakia & agapi,
George Dimitrios Calombaris

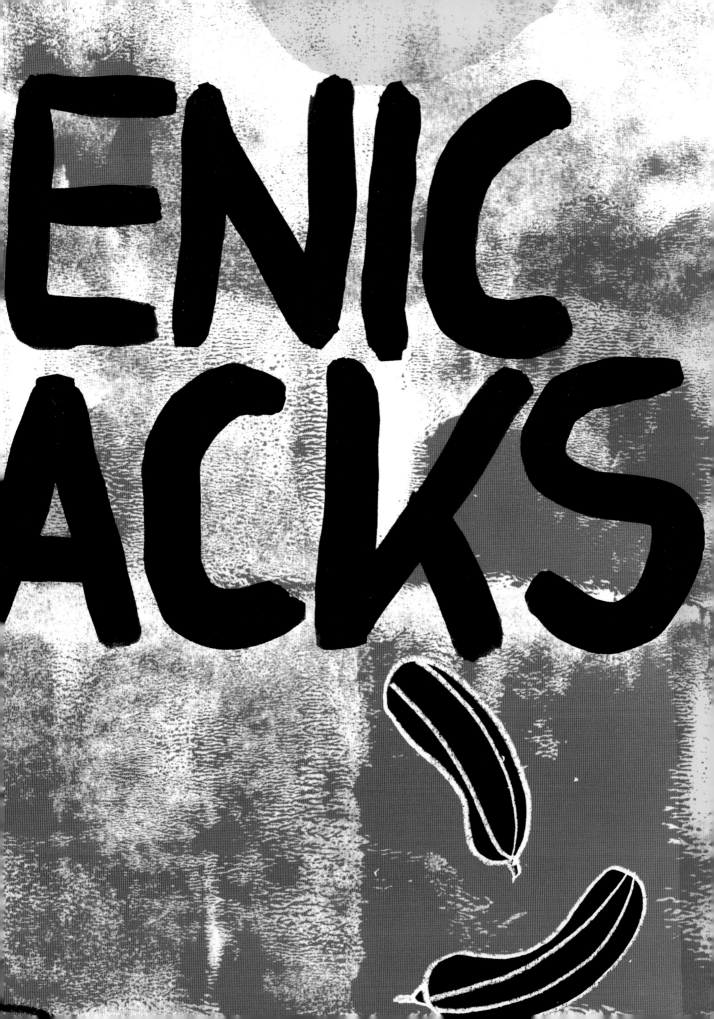

Serves 4

200 ml pure cream (45% fat)
300 g feta
100 ml full-cream milk
2 teaspoons dried mint

Heirloom carrot salad
1 bunch heirloom
   baby yellow carrots
1 bunch heirloom
   baby purple carrots
1 bunch heirloom
   baby orange carrots
2 small radishes, very thinly sliced
extra virgin olive oil, for drizzling
3 sprigs oregano, leaves picked
salt flakes and cracked pepper

Whipped feta, heirloom carrot salad

This is a dish that I love to eat with my little ones. It's crisp, it's healthy and it's yum. My kids don't eat fast food – I teach them that food should be whole and real. There is no other way.

Whip the cream in a medium bowl until soft peaks form.

Place the feta, milk and dried mint in another bowl and blend with a stick blender until smooth. Using a rubber spatula, fold the blended feta into the cream.

To make the salad, peel the baby carrots using a vegetable peeler and trim the leaves. Cut the carrots in half lengthways. Place in a bowl with the radish and drizzle with olive oil. Add the oregano leaves and season to taste with salt and pepper, then gently toss to combine.

Serve the salad with the whipped feta, finished with a final drizzle of olive oil.

Makes 20

20 baby qukes
1 bunch dill
2 cups (500 ml) champagne
  vinegar
1 tablespoon honey
20 coriander seeds
3 star anise
3 tablespoons table salt
10 cardamom pods
10 white peppercorns
½ cup (125 ml) ouzo

Pickled Cucumbers
–ouzaki mezathaki

My dad is a meze man, so this little dish reminds me of him. I really don't think it's about what you give him but more the sense of occasion. Eating food is and always should be an occasion. This one is all about enjoying an afternoon snack in the sun with lots of ouzo. You can find the qukes (baby cucumbers) in most good supermarkets.

Pinprick the qukes all over about a dozen times (or use a small knife) and place in a large jar with a lid.

Remove the sprigs from the dill stalks, then place the stalks in a saucepan, reserving the sprigs. Add the remaining ingredients, except the qukes, to the pan, pour in 2 cups (500 ml) water and bring to the boil.

Pour the boiling liquid through a fine sieve over the qukes, then seal the jar with its lid and set aside to cool. Once cooled, place in the fridge until needed. Stored this way, they will keep for up to 2 weeks. Serve garnished with the reserved sprigs.

Serves 4

70 ml extra virgin olive oil
4 × 80 g slices kefalograviera

Cumquat and currant glyko
300 g cumquats
1 teaspoon black mustard seeds
1 teaspoon yellow mustard seeds
50 g currants
40 g caster sugar
⅓ cup (80 ml) chardonnay vinegar

Saganaki, cumquat, currant glyko

It really bothers me that saganaki has been messed about with over the years to the point where it completely misrepresents Hellenic food. Time for a rethink. Glyko is a classic Greek spoon sweet but here I have made it savoury to go with the saganaki. It's all about salty cheese and a sweet glyko with acidity. The glyko can be made ahead and kept in a jar until you need it – just make sure you warm it up before serving. The most important thing about this recipe is to make sure you eat the cheese while it is hot.

To make the cumquat and currant glyko, place the cumquats in a medium saucepan and cover with cold water. Bring to the boil over high heat, then strain, discarding the water. Repeat this process twice more, replacing the water each time. On the final boil, add the remaining ingredients and and simmer gently for 15–20 minutes or until most of the liquid has evaporated.

Heat the olive oil in a non-stick frying pan over medium heat. When hot, add the cheese slices and cook for 2 minutes each side or until golden and soft to touch.

To serve, place the fried cheese on a hot plate and spoon over the warm glyko. Serve immediately.

Serves 4

100 g kataifi pastry
100 ml extra virgin olive oil
4 large raw king prawns, peeled
   and deveined, tails intact
1 ripe avocado
2 litres cottonseed oil
salt flakes
coriander leaves, to garnish

Honey dressing
1 teaspoon coriander seeds
1 tablespoon lime juice
2 tablespoons fish sauce
80 g honey
¼ cup (20 g) almonds, toasted

Kataifi prawns, honey dressing, avocado

A little tip for you here is to make sure you bring the kataifi pastry to room temperature before you use it. You can buy it from all good Mediterranean delis. For golden, crisp prawns cook them in batches so you don't bring down the temperature of the oil.

Pull the pastry apart and arrange into four 15 cm lengths. Brush with the olive oil, then wrap each prawn in pastry and refrigerate for 1 hour.

To make the honey dressing, toast the coriander seeds in a dry frying pan, then transfer to a mortar and pestle and lightly crush them. Place in a small bowl, add the lime juice, fish sauce, honey and almonds and whisk to combine.

Shortly before you are ready to serve, cut the avocado in half and remove the skin and seed. Cut each half in half again, then cut each piece lengthways into three slices.

Heat the cottonseed oil in a deep-fryer to 180°C (or in a heavy-based saucepan until a cube of bread browns in 15 seconds). Add the pastry-wrapped prawns and cook for 3 minutes or until golden and cooked through. Remove with a slotted spoon and drain on paper towel. Season with salt flakes.

Arrange the prawns and avocado on a serving plate, dress with the honey dressing and garnish with coriander leaves.

Note
If you would prefer not to deep-fry the prawns, you can bake them instead. Preheat the oven to 200°C (fan-forced). Place the chilled, wrapped prawns on a baking tray lined with baking paper and bake for 10 minutes or until golden. Check that they are cooked through, then sprinkle with salt flakes and serve as above.

Serves 4

2 star anise
2 tablespoons salt flakes
2 litres vegetable oil
1 bunch kale

Kale chips, Star anise salt

These little gems make a great snack with ice-cold beer, but they also add a really nice flavour and texture to salads. For the very best results, make sure you season the chips with the star anise salt as soon as you remove them from the oil.

Grind the star anise to a fine powder in a mortar and pestle. Add the salt flakes and mix well.

Heat the vegetable oil in a deep-fryer to 150°C (or in a heavy-based saucepan until a cube of bread browns in 30 seconds).

Meanwhile, remove the kale from the stalk and cut into bite-sized pieces, keeping the leaves as chunky as possible. Wash and dry well.

Add the kale to the oil in batches and cook for 2 minutes or until crisp but still bright green. Remove with a slotted spoon and drain on paper towel. Season with the star anise salt and serve immediately.

Serves 4

⅓ cup (50 g) cornflour
1 teaspoon cayenne pepper
1 teaspoon fennel seeds, crushed
1 tablespoon coriander seeds,
   crushed
1 teaspoon salt flakes
½ teaspoon cracked pepper
2 litres cottonseed oil
4 quail, butterflied, ribcage
   removed (ask your butcher
   to do this for you)
extra virgin olive oil, to garnish

Beetroot tzatziki
1 large beetroot
salt flakes
1 clove garlic
100 g hung yoghurt (see page 42)
juice of 1 lemon
2½ tablespoons extra virgin
   olive oil
¼ bunch coriander, leaves picked
   and roughly chopped
½ bunch dill, fronds picked
   and roughly chopped
cracked pepper

Crispy quail, beetroot tzatziki

This was on my very first menu: Press Club 2006. I still love it as it's really tasty and looks amazing, but is easy to achieve. The beetroot dip is also a nice little condiment to go with bread.

Preheat the oven to 180°C (fan-forced).

To make the beetroot tzatziki, lightly season the beetroot with salt, then wrap it in foil and bake for 35 minutes or until tender enough to push a skewer through. Wrap the garlic clove in foil and add to the oven. Roast with the beetroot for a further 10 minutes. Set aside to cool. Grate the cooled beetroot with a box grater, then wrap in a J-cloth or square of muslin, place in a sieve over a bowl and squeeze out any excess juice.

Blitz the beetroot, garlic and yoghurt in a food processor until very smooth. Add the lemon juice and olive oil and blitz again. Tip the mixture into a bowl and fold in the coriander and dill. Season to taste with salt and pepper.

Mix together the cornflour, cayenne pepper, fennel and coriander seeds, salt and pepper in a shallow bowl.

Heat the cottonseed oil in a deep-fryer to 180°C (or in a heavy-based saucepan until a cube of bread browns in 15 seconds).

Cut the quail in half, then toss in the cornflour seasoning, shaking off any excess. Add to the hot oil in batches and cook for 3–4 minutes or until cooked through and golden brown.

Remove the quail and drain on paper towel, then serve with the beetroot tzatziki and a drizzle of olive oil.

Serves 4

100 g white salted cod roe
70 ml vegetable oil
100 g unsalted butter
½ cup (120 g) popcorn kernels

Taramosalata-flavoured popcorn

I remember making this for the first time at Gazi and getting my team to taste it. They all laughed, so I knew it was a winner. Food is there to warm us through and make us feel happy – we can go to the dentist if we want to be miserable.

Place the cod roe and 2½ tablespoons vegetable oil in a medium frying pan with a lid. Cook over low heat, stirring frequently, until golden brown. Add the butter and cook further until caramelised. Set aside.

Pour the remaining oil into a deep saucepan with a lid and place over low heat. Add the popcorn kernels and stir. Make sure you put a lid on it! Let the kernels pop, shaking the pan often.

Remove from the heat. Add the tarama butter and toss to coat well. Serve hot.

Makes 8

2½ tablespoons pomegranate
 molasses
40 g sesame seeds
salt flakes
good-quality olives and butter
 sprinkled with salt flakes or
 black Greek salt, to serve

Koulourakia dough
3 teaspoons dried yeast
2 cups (300 g) plain flour
1 teaspoon table salt
1 teaspoon caster sugar
270 g plain flour, extra
1 teaspoon table salt, extra

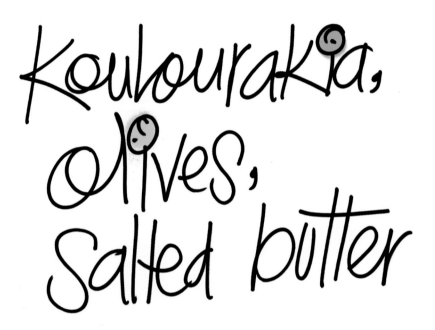

Koulourakia, olives, Salted butter

I love the fact that to this day there are single industries in Athens. The sock man sells the socks, and the mushroom lady sells the mushrooms. When I was in Athens, I would visit the platia (square) every morning and buy a koulouraki. The round piece of bread, crusted in seasame seeds, was a little bit chewy but so good. I found it incredibly inspiring to walk through the ancient city eating such humble traditional food. Start this recipe the night before so the dough can prove slowly in the fridge.

To make the koulourakia dough, dissolve the yeast in 400 ml tepid water, then combine in a large bowl with flour, salt and sugar and knead until smooth. Cover and set aside in the fridge overnight. The next day, add the extra flour and salt and knead until incorporated.

Preheat the oven to 180°C (fan-forced). Line a large baking tray with baking paper.

Divide the dough into eight portions. Using the palm of your hand, roll each portion into a 40 cm long rope. Bring the two ends together, twisting to join them and form a circle.

Combine the pomegranate molasses and 2½ tablespoons water in a small bowl.

Place the koulourakia on a baking tray and brush with pomegranate glaze. Sprinkle with the sesame seeds and a little salt.

Bake for 15–20 minutes or until nicely golden. Serve hot with olives and salted butter.

Serves 12

1 teaspoon dried yeast
1⅔ cups (250 g) plain flour,
    plus extra for dusting
1 tablespoon honey
1 teaspoon extra virgin olive oil
1 teaspoon table salt
1 egg, lightly beaten with
    1 teaspoon water
fennel seeds, sesame seeds and
    salt flakes, for sprinkling

Greek salad salsa
1 red onion, finely diced
1 red capsicum (pepper),
    finely diced
1 green capsicum (pepper),
    finely diced

1 tomato, finely diced
2 stavros peppers (see page 34),
    finely diced
½ Lebanese cucumber,
    finely diced
8 black pitted olives, roughly
    chopped
1 tablespoon salted baby
    capers, rinsed
about 20 oregano leaves
2 teaspoons balsamic vinegar
1 tablespoon extra virgin olive oil
salt flakes and cracked pepper
100 g feta, crumbled
nasturtium leaves, to garnish
    (optional)

Crispy fennel-seed flatbread, Greek Salad Salsa

This thin, crisp bread is super light and totally delicious. The salsa that goes with it needs to be freshly made – don't let it sit around for too long or it will go soggy. Having said that, all the juices in the bottom of the bowl are great with bread; in fact, they're my dad's favourite part of any salad (see page 219). Geez he's a wise man.

Dissolve the dried yeast in 85 ml tepid water in a large bowl. Leave in a warm place for 15–20 minutes or until it activates and small bubbles form. Add the flour, honey, olive oil and salt and knead to form a smooth dough. Shape the dough into a flat disc in the bowl and cover with plastic film, then rest in the fridge for at least 1 hour.

Divide the dough into 12 portions. Using a pasta machine if you have one (or a rolling pin if you don't), roll out each piece of dough with a little bit of flour to a 3 mm thickness.

Preheat the oven to 180°C (conventional). You don't want fan-forced for this recipe. Line two or three large baking trays with baking paper.

Place the dough sheets on the prepared trays and brush with the egg wash. Sprinkle the fennel seeds, sesame seeds and salt flakes over the top and bake for 8–10 minutes or until crisp and golden. Remove and allow to cool.

To make the salsa, mix together the diced vegetables, olives, capers and oregano. Combine the balsamic vinegar and olive oil and pour over the salad. Season to taste and gently toss to combine. Transfer to a bowl or shallow plate and scatter the feta and nasturtium leaves (if using) over the top.

Serve the flatbread with the Greek salad salsa.

Serves 4

1 tablespoon extra virgin olive oil
200 g stavros peppers or any
    small variety of chilli
1¼ tablespoons sherry vinegar
salt flakes and cracked pepper
30 g feta, crumbled

Pine-nut crunch
10 g butter, melted
⅓ cup (25 g) panko breadcrumbs
1 heaped tablespoon pine nuts
finely grated zest of ¼ lemon
salt flakes

Stavros peppers, feta, sherry vinegar, pine-nut crunch

We named these Stavros peppers because a man by the name of Stavros grows them for us in northern Queensland. In Greece you would find similar peppers in Florina, and I guess that's where the idea for the dish comes from. It's important that the peppers are cooked so they become nice and sweet.

Preheat the oven to 160°C (fan-forced). Line a baking tray with baking paper.

To make the pine-nut crunch, mix together the melted butter and breadcrumbs. Spread out on the prepared baking tray and bake for 10 minutes. Add the pine nuts and bake for a further 10 minutes or until golden. Sprinkle over the lemon zest and salt to taste, then set aside to cool.

Heat the olive oil in a frying pan over medium–high heat, add the peppers and cook until they blister. Pour in the sherry vinegar to deglaze the pan and season with salt and pepper.

Serve the pepper mixture straight away with the crumbled feta and the pine-nut crunch.

MY MUM'S CHICKEN NUGGETS

– WHERE ALL IS NOT AS IT SEEMS

As an Aussie Greek boy growing up in an ethnic family all I wanted was to be like my next-door neighbours. I wanted to dress like them, act like them and have my mum cook food like them. One of the dishes I most wanted Mum to make was chicken nuggets. Yep, chicken nuggets. So Mum said no problem and busied herself in the kitchen. For years we loved our mum's chicken nuggets until one day we discovered that they were in fact lamb brains! Crispy and crunchy on the outside and beautifully creamy on the inside. At first I was outraged, but in the end I was grateful that my mother cooks with whole and real food. I can't wait for my kids to ask me to cook them chicken nuggets!

We should all be eating this forgotten meat. Brains are super healthy and, when cooked well, they're absolutely delicious. I love to serve them with a little tartare sauce or sometimes just a squeeze of lemon juice. Make sure you soak them overnight in water first to clean them thoroughly.

I'm a firm believer that we must eat from nose to tail. The animal has been sacrificed for us and we must respect it as chefs and customers by using every bit. We waste far too much food in Australia. My mum taught us this valuable lesson as we were growing up – she always found a way to make things last and never threw anything out. It's so simple really. I guess when you have had struggles in your life (like my mum) you don't take anything for granted. Respect your friends, respect your food and where it came from and, above all, don't take anything for granted.

Crispy lamb brains, burnt leek cream, pickled grapes

Serves 4

4 lamb brains
2 teaspoons dried oregano
salt flakes
⅔ cup (100 g) plain flour
2 eggs, lightly beaten
100 g panko breadcrumbs
vegetable oil, for deep-frying
4 sprigs dill
nasturtium leaves,
   to garnish (optional)
extra virgin olive oil, to serve

Burnt leek cream
1 leek
25 g butter
½ onion, finely diced
150 ml pure cream (35% fat)
¼ teaspoon dried oregano

Pickled grapes
12 seedless red grapes,
   cut in half
12 seedless green grapes,
   cut in half
2½ tablespoons white
   wine vinegar
50 g caster sugar

Trim any excess connective tissue from the lamb brains, then remove the membrane and cut them in half. Steam the brains in a steamer or double boiler for 6 minutes, then refresh immediately in iced water. Remove the brains from the water and pat dry with paper towel.

Season the brains with oregano and salt, and lightly dust with flour. Dip them in the beaten egg, then coat in panko breadcrumbs, shaking off any excess. Set aside in the fridge until needed.

For the burnt leek cream, preheat a barbecue grill or flatplate to high heat and preheat the oven to 170°C (fan-forced). Split the leek in half lengthways and wash thoroughly, removing the green end and the outer layer. Place on a baking tray and bake for 25 minutes. Remove from the oven and char on the grill until blackened. Allow to cool, then cut into 1 cm pieces. Melt the butter in a small saucepan over medium–low heat, add the onion and cook until translucent. Add the leek and pour in the cream. Bring to the boil, then reduce the heat and simmer for 5 minutes. Set aside.

For the pickled grapes, place the grapes in a small heatproof container. Bring the vinegar and sugar to the boil until the sugar has dissolved, then pour over the grapes. Cover with a lid and allow to cool.

Shortly before you are ready to serve, heat the oil for deep-frying in a deep-fryer to 180°C (or in a heavy-based saucepan until a cube of bread browns in 15 seconds). Add the lamb brains and cook until golden (about 4–5 minutes). Remove with a slotted spoon and drain on paper towel. Season with salt flakes.

Warm the leek cream and stir in the oregano, then spoon onto serving plates. Top with the crisp lamb brains and pickled grapes and garnish with dill sprigs, nasturtium leaves (if using) and a drizzle of olive oil.

Serves 4

250 g natural yoghurt
1 clove garlic, unpeeled
200 g carrots
½ teaspoon salt flakes
1 teaspoon honey
⅛ teaspoon cayenne
  pepper (optional)

finely grated zest of 1 lemon
2 tablespoons lemon juice
1 tablespoon natural
  yoghurt, extra
extra virgin olive oil, for drizzling
crispy fennel-seed flatbread
  (see page 32), to serve

This dip is made with some pretty simple ingredients, but it is so important to roast your garlic before you use it. Roasting removes the astringent flavour that can be a little overpowering. There is nothing worse than going out for meal and tasting it again the next day, if you know what I mean.

Place the yoghurt in the centre of a clean J-cloth or square of muslin. Bring the corners together and tie securely with string, then place in a sieve with a bowl underneath to catch any liquid. Drain in the fridge overnight. The hung yoghurt is now ready to use.

Preheat the oven to 180°C (fan-forced). Wrap the garlic clove in foil and roast for 10–15 minutes or until soft. Allow to cool, then remove the skin.

Wash and peel the carrots, then finely grate. Season with the salt and set aside for 15 minutes, then place in the centre of a clean J-cloth or square of muslin and wring out any excess moisture.

Measure out 75 g of the hung yoghurt and combine in a bowl with the carrot, garlic, honey, cayenne pepper (if using), lemon zest, lemon juice and extra yoghurt. Leftover hung yoghurt can be used to make other dips, such as the beetroot tzatziki on page 24.

Transfer the tzatziki to a bowl and drizzle with a little olive oil. Serve with crispy flatbread.

Serves 4

1 cup (200 g) dried yellow
    split peas
½ brown onion, roughly chopped
1 small carrot, roughly chopped
1 clove garlic, roughly chopped
extra virgin olive oil, to taste
salt flakes
white truffle oil, to taste
raw baby vegetables, peeled and
    washed, to serve

Dressing
2 spring onions, thinly sliced
2 tablespoons salted baby
    capers, rinsed
1 tablespoon shredded
    flat-leaf parsley
1 tablespoon vinegar sherry
1 tablespoon extra virgin olive oil

Fava, white truffle oil, capers, spring onion

As a general rule I don't really like truffle oil. Truffles don't contain any oil so it doesn't make sense to me. But you know what? With this recipe I'll make an exception. This dip is great vego dish, and it's the truffle oil that makes it so special. To really taste all the flavours, serve it at room temperature rather than cold from the fridge.

Soak the split peas in cold water overnight.

Drain the soaked peas, then place in a saucepan of fresh water and bring to the boil. Drain and return to the pan with the onion, carrot and garlic. Pour in enough water to cover by 2–3 cm. Bring to the boil, skimming off any froth on the surface, then reduce the heat and simmer for 15–20 minutes or until the split peas are tender but not overcooked. Drain, then place in a blender while still warm and blend with a good splash of olive oil until smooth. Season to taste with salt and truffle oil.

Cover the fava closely with plastic film to prevent a skin forming and leave to cool completely. Blend again to adjust the consistency if needed – you want it to be silky smooth.

To make the dressing, combine all the ingredients in a small bowl.

Pour the dressing over the fava and serve with raw baby vegetables.

Serves 4

1 tablespoon extra virgin olive oil blended with 1 tablespoon vegetable oil
5 cloves garlic, thinly sliced
1 spring onion, thinly sliced
½ head cauliflower, very finely chopped
100 ml milk
100 ml pure cream (45% fat)
1¼ tablespoons sherry vinegar
salt flakes
grilled pita bread (see page 289), to serve

Crispy pork

1 tablespoon extra virgin olive oil blended with 1 tablespoon vegetable oil
120 g minced pork
¼ brown onion, finely diced
1 clove garlic, finely diced
⅛ teaspoon five-spice powder
2 tablespoons sherry vinegar
salt flakes

Cauliflower Skordalia, Crispy pork

Okay, I admit the inspiration for this recipe came from a little Armenian restaurant in Dubai, where they served a hummus dip with crispy basturma on top. I thought it was delicious, but have reworked the idea to make it my own. Remember, its fine to take inspiration but so important to pay homage.

Heat the oil blend in a medium saucepan over medium heat, add the garlic, spring onion and cauliflower and cook gently until softened. Add the milk and cream and bring to the boil, then reduce the heat and simmer for 15–20 minutes or until half the liquid has evaporated. Remove from the heat and cool slightly, then puree with a stick blender (or in a food processor) until smooth. Stir in the sherry vinegar and season to taste with salt.

To make the crispy pork, heat the oil blend in a frying pan over medium–high heat and saute the pork for 5–8 minutes, breaking up any lumps with a wooden spoon. Add the onion and garlic and cook for a further 5 minutes or until translucent. By now the pork mixture should be well caramelised. Stir in the five-spice powder and deglaze the pan with the sherry vinegar. Season to taste with salt.

Sprinkle the crispy pork over the skordalia and and serve with grilled pita bread.

Serves 4

about 120 g crustless bread
  (I like ciabatta)
¼ brown onion, finely diced
175 g white tarama paste
2½ tablespoons extra virgin
  olive oil blended with
    2½ tablespoons vegetable oil
⅓ cup (80 ml) lemon juice
salt flakes and cracked pepper
vegetable oil, for deep-frying
16–20 prawn crackers
extra virgin olive oil, to garnish

Taramosalata, prawn crackers

For me, tarama (to use its Grenglish name) is the Hellenic umami – it has so much flavour and needs little embellishment. Let the natural ingredients speak for themselves and your taramosalata will be white, not pink. This is absolutely how it should be – I am passionate about this! You can buy salted white cod roe from specialised delis.

The prawn crackers are a whimsical touch. Of course they add texture, but they remind me of buying prawn crackers from our local Chinese restaurant in Mulgrave when we were kids. Ahhh, love a bit of nostalgia.

Soak the bread in a bowl of water for 2–3 minutes or until soft. Squeeze out any excess water and check the weight – you'll need 120 g soaked bread.

Place the bread, onion and tarama in a blender and blend to a fine puree. With the motor running, slowly add the oil blend to thicken the dip. Add the lemon juice and season to taste with salt and pepper.

Heat the oil for deep-frying in a deep-fryer to 180°C (or in a heavy-based saucepan until a cube of bread browns in 15 seconds). Add the prawn crackers in batches and cook for 10–15 seconds or until puffed up. Remove with a slotted spoon and drain on paper towel. Allow to cool completely.

Drizzle a little olive oil over the taramosalata and serve with the prawn crackers.

Serves 4

200 g dried chickpeas
1 clove garlic, unpeeled
1 teaspoon coriander seeds,
  plus extra to garnish (optional)
50 g roasted salted peanuts
1 tablespoon tahini
75 ml extra virgin olive oil blended
  with 75 ml vegetable oil
juice of ½ lemon
salt flakes
extra virgin olive oil, to garnish
grilled pita bread (see page 289),
  to serve

Peanut and coriander-seed hummus

I have always loved peanut butter. When I was growing up I would have it on my toast every single morning. So incorporating peanuts into hummus wasn't much of a leap, and the results are delicious. Make sure you toast off your coriander seeds first.

Soak the chickpeas in water overnight. Drain, then cook in fresh water (without any salt) until tender. Leave to cool completely in the liquid.

Preheat the oven to 180°C (fan-forced). Wrap the garlic clove in foil and roast for 10–15 minutes or until soft. Allow to cool, then remove the skin.

Meanwhile, toast the coriander seeds in a dry frying pan, then transfer to a mortar and pestle and crush to a fine powder.

Drain the chickpeas, reserving a little of the cooking water. Place in a food processor with the garlic, ground coriander, peanuts, tahini and oil blend and blend to a smooth paste. Stir in the lemon juice and season to taste with salt. If the dip is too thick, add a little of the reserved cooking liquid to thin it down.

Transfer the hummus to a bowl and garnish with olive oil and coriander seeds (if using). Serve with grilled pita bread.

Serves 4

2 medium eggplants (aubergines)
50 g white miso paste
2½ tablespoons extra virgin
   olive oil blended with
   2½ tablespoons vegetable oil
brown sugar, for sprinkling
2 cloves garlic, crushed
juice of ½ lemon
salt flakes
yoghurt, capers and sliced radish,
   to garnish (optional)
grilled pita bread (see page 289),
   to serve

Miso Melitzanosalata

Miso? Greek? Of course
... *not!* But why not take
influences from one cuisine
and incorporate them into
another? The unique flavour
of miso intensifies an otherwise
simple eggplant dip, making
a super-healthy snack for adults
and kids alike, or serve it as
a puree under a simply
cooked piece of fish.

Preheat the oven to 180°C (fan-forced) and line a baking tray with baking paper.

Using a sharp knife, remove the top and skin from the eggplants, then cut into 5 cm dice. Place in a bowl with the miso paste and oil blend and mix well. Spread out on the prepared tray and sprinkle lightly with brown sugar. Roast for 10–15 minutes or until golden and tender.

Allow the eggplant to cool slightly, then place in a food processor with the garlic and blend until smooth. Stir in the lemon and season to taste with salt. Spoon into a bowl and garnish with yoghurt, capers and sliced radish (if using). Serve with pita bread.

Serves 4

2 small beetroots
2 tablespoons milk
80 g feta, plus extra to garnish
finely grated zest of 1 lemon
juice of ¼ lemon
1¼ tablespoons extra virgin
   olive oil
salt flakes and cracked pepper
oregano leaves, to garnish
crispy fennel-seed flatbread
   (see page 32) or village bread
   (see page 288), to serve

Beetroot and feta dip

In Greece, beetroots are a lunchtime staple in the summer time, cooked simply and dressed just with olive oil and salt. From this I began to develop an idea for a dip, but it wasn't until I included feta that it all came together. I mean, what would the world be without feta?

Preheat the oven to 180°C (fan-forced).

Wash the beetroots well to remove any dirt, then wrap them in foil and bake for 1 hour or until very soft. Allow to cool, then remove the skin.

Place in a sieve lined with a clean J-cloth or a square of muslin, with a bowl underneath to catch any liquid. Drain in the fridge overnight.

The next day, squeeze out any remaining juice from the beetroot and place in a blender.

Using a stick blender, blend the milk and feta until smooth. Add the mixture to the beetroot, along with the lemon zest, lemon juice and olive oil. Season to taste with salt and pepper and blend until smooth. Sprinkle with oregano leves and extra feta, and serve with fresh bread.

Serves 4

400 g dried white beans
200 g raw chicken skin
4 cloves garlic, unpeeled
200 ml extra virgin olive oil,
    plus extra to garnish
¼ cup (60 ml) white
    wine vinegar
2 teaspoons salt flakes
black Cypriot salt,
    to garnish (optional)

White bean skordalia, crispy chicken skin

A classic skordalia is made simply with garlic and potato. Adding white beans, such as cannellini, makes it into a nutritious and tasty dip, but it's also really great served with roast pork. Ask your butcher for the chicken skin.

Soak the white beans in water overnight. Drain, then cook in fresh water (without any salt) until tender. Leave to cool completely in the liquid.

Preheat the oven to 200°C (fan-forced) and line a baking tray with baking paper.

Place the chicken skin on a cutting board. Using a sharp knife, scrape any excess fat from the inside of the skin, taking care to keep the skin intact. Transfer the skin to the prepared tray and lay it out flat. Top with another sheet of baking paper and press down with a second baking tray. Bake for 5–10 minutes or until crisp and golden. Cool completely, then store in an airtight container until needed.

Reduce the oven temperature to 180°C (fan-forced). Wrap the garlic cloves in foil and roast for 10–15 minutes or until soft. Allow to cool, then remove the skin.

Drain the beans, then place in a food processor with the garlic and olive oil and blend until smooth. Stir in the vinegar and season to taste with salt.

Spread out the skordalia on a plate and drizzle over a little olive oil. Garnish with black salt (if using) and serve with the crispy chicken skin.

Serves 4

200 g feta
200 g natural Greek-style yoghurt
1 tablespoon dried mint
juice of ½ lemon
2 tablespoons finely chopped dill
raw baby vegetables, peeled and
    washed if necessary, to serve

Feta, yoghurt and dried mint dip

A Hellenic kitchen without feta is like a fisherman without a fishing rod. Feta is eaten all day long, for breakfast, lunch and dinner. You're simply not Greek if you don't eat feta. Okay, I think I've made the point. If you love feta, you'll love this dip. Just make sure you don't season it with too much salt as the feta is already pretty salty.

Place the feta, yoghurt, mint and lemon juice in a food processor and blend until smooth.

Fold through the dill just before serving. This is delicious served with raw baby vegetables.

Serves 4

600 g brown onions, peeled
  and cut into quarters
1 clove garlic, peeled and
  left whole
2½ tablespoons extra virgin
  olive oil
1 tablespoon roughly chopped
  flat-leaf parsley

¼ teaspoon salt flakes
juice of 1 lemon
50 g goat's curd
1 heaped tablespoon
  bonito flakes
rice crackers or village bread
  (see page 288), to serve

Burnt onion and goat's curd dip, bonito flakes

There is nothing Greek about this recipe, but I guess you could say that about me too – an Aussie boy growing up in Melbourne. But of course being Greek is not just about being born there – it's a state of mind (and heart and soul). To me it's simple: this dip is completely yum. And in my language yum is king. So that's that. You can buy bonito flakes from all good Asian shops.

Preheat the oven to 200°C (fan-forced) and line a baking tray with baking paper.

Place the onion, garlic and 1½ tablespoons olive oil in a bowl and toss to coat well. Transfer to the prepared tray and roast for 13–15 minutes or until the onion is slightly black on the tips. Remove and allow to cool, then roughly chop.

Heat the remaining olive oil in a frying pan over low heat and gently saute the onion mixture for 15 minutes.

While still warm, transfer the onion mixture to a food processor, add the parsley and salt and blend to a puree. Stir in the lemon juice, then transfer to a bowl and top with the goat's curd and bonito flakes. Serve with rice crackers or fresh bread.

A DELICATE BROTH TO NOURISH AND NURTURE

This delicate dish has always been close to my heart. I truly believe that food can cure us, and whenever I am feeling unwell the thought of this beautiful bowl of goodness makes me feel so much better. It's the simplest of soups but of course this means you have nowhere to hide. The chicken stock is what holds it all together and it needs to be homemade and full of flavour. Makes sure you don't ruin it by overboiling it – a gentle dish like this needs a light touch.

I remember when I was growing up we'd be driving down the highway and Mum would make Dad pull over when she spotted wild greens growing by the side of the road. I would be so embarrassed as I was certain people were staring at these strange people collecting weeds. In fact, those 'weeds' were chicory, endive and kale, which we all now know taste amazing and are so good for you. There is a reason why the Ikarians have lived for so long, I guess. The Hellenic diet is so good for you.

Avgolemono, haloumi

Serves 2

2 cups (500 ml) chicken stock (see page 298)
4 eggs, lightly beaten
1 tablespoon salt flakes
1 teaspoon finely chopped dill
150 g haloumi
2–2½ tablespoons lemon juice
extra virgin olive oil, to garnish

Place the stock, egg and salt in a saucepan over medium–low heat. Whisking constantly, bring the temperature to 80–85°C, which will cook the eggs and thicken the soup. Once it reaches this point, remove the pan from the heat and add the dill. Cut 50 g of the haloumi into 1 cm dice and add to the soup to warm through.

Cut the remaining haloumi into two slices and pan-fry on both sides. Season the soup with lemon juice and finish with a drizzle of olive oil. Serve immediately with the haloumi.

Serves 4–6

1.25 litres chicken stock
  (see page 298)
500 g dried kritharaki (orzo) pasta
150 g butter
large handful of flat-leaf parsley,
  roughly chopped
½ bunch chives, chopped into
  3 cm lengths
salt flakes and cracked pepper
1¼ cups (100 g) grated parmesan

Chicken meatballs
200 g skinless chicken breast
  fillet, finely minced
200 g skinless chicken thigh fillet,
  finely minced
1 cup (70 g) fresh breadcrumbs
2 eggs
1 cup (80 g) grated parmesan
large handful of flat-leaf parsley,
  roughly chopped
1 tablespoon finely
  chopped thyme

Chicken Kritharaki

I am very lucky to have a grandmother of Italian heritage, which meant I grew up enjoying the best of both worlds. Like many pasta dishes, this is warm and comforting. It should have a nice wet texture and is definitely designed to be eaten with a spoon.

To make the chicken meatballs, place all the ingredients in a bowl and mix well with your hands until well combined (use prep gloves for this). Roll level tablespoons of the mixture into balls.

Pour 400 ml chicken stock into a large saucepan and bring to a simmer. Add the meatballs and gently poach for 8–10 minutes or until cooked through.

Meanwhile, pour the remaining stock into a separate saucepan and bring to the boil. Add the pasta and cook for 12–14 minutes or until al dente. Fold in the butter, parsley and chives, then toss through the meatballs and season to taste with salt and pepper. Finish with a generous scattering of parmesan.

Serves 4

extra virgin olive oil, for pan-frying
   and tossing
4 duck legs
½ brown onion, finely diced
1 small carrot, finely diced
½ leek, white part only,
   finely diced
1 stick celery, finely diced
2 cloves garlic, finely chopped
1 cup (250 ml) dry white wine
2 ripe tomatoes, roughly chopped
400 ml chicken stock
   (see page 298)
200 g broad beans, blanched
   and peeled
1 teaspoon dried mint
30 g butter

Hilopites pasta
1⅔ cups (250 g) type '00' flour,
   plus extra for dusting
½ teaspoon salt flakes
1 egg
4 large egg yolks
2 teaspoons extra virgin olive oil

Hilopites, duck, broad beans

Hilopites are classic Cretan
pasta strips, often served
simply with melted butter and
cheese. They also work well
with a more robust sauce, and
here I have added duck and
broad beans, both of which
I love. Double-shell the broad
beans if they are large, but
once will do if they're small.

Preheat the oven to 120°C (fan-forced). Heat a little olive oil in a flameproof
casserole dish over medium heat. Add the ducks legs and cook until
browned all over. Remove. Add the onion, carrot, leek, celery and garlic
and saute until golden brown. Return the duck legs to the pan and
deglaze with the white wine. Add the tomato and stock, then cover with
a lid and gently braise in the oven for 3 hours.

Meanwhile, to make the pasta dough, blend all the ingredients in a food
processor until the mixture resembles fine breadcrumbs. Tip into a large
bowl and knead for 2 minutes. Cover the bowl with plastic film and rest
for 1 hour at room temperature.

Cut the dough in half and wrap one portion in plastic film. Pass the
other portion of dough through a pasta machine on the thickest setting.
To laminate the dough, fold it in half lengthways and pass it through the
machine on the thickest setting, folded end first. Repeat this step three
times for each portion of dough.

Once laminated, pass each pasta sheet through the machine on
each setting until you reach the second thinnest setting, using a little
flour to prevent sticking. Cut the pasta into 6 cm × 2 cm strips.

Shortly before you are ready to serve, cook the pasta in boiling
salted water for 2–3 minutes or until al dente. Drain and toss with
1½ tablespoons olive oil. Set aside.

Remove the duck legs from the casserole dish, then strain the sauce
and set aside. Separate the duck meat from the bones and return it
to the pan. Discard the bones.

Reheat the sauce if necessary, add the broad beans and cook for
2 minutes. Add the pasta and stir gently so it absorbs some of the
sauce. Finally, stir through the dried mint and butter and serve.

Serves 4

The pasta dough is made from a traditional Cypriot recipe, but the filling is so not classic. Please take note: there is a difference between burnt and BURNT. The filling needs to take on the sweetness of charred leeks, not ash, so be super careful.

For a touch of luxury, spoon a little cauliflower skordalia (see page 46) on the bottom of the plate and top the pasta with shaved truffle.

2 leeks
semolina, for dusting
2 tablespoons finely chopped dill
30 g fresh breadcrumbs
1 egg
100 g feta
½ bunch chives, finely chopped
2 egg yolks, lightly beaten
⅔ cup (160 ml) extra virgin
　olive oil

30 g feta, extra, crumbled
100 g almonds, toasted and
　roughly chopped

Egg pasta
2 eggs
1⅓ cups (200 g) type '00' flour,
　plus extra for dusting
1 teaspoon extra virgin olive oil
¼ teaspoon salt flakes

To make the pasta dough, blend all the ingredients in a food processor until the mixture resembles fine breadcrumbs. Tip into a large bowl and knead for 2 minutes. Cover the bowl with plastic film and rest for 1 hour at room temperature.

Cut the dough in half and wrap one portion in plastic film. Pass the other portion of dough through a pasta machine on the thickest setting. To laminate the dough, fold it in half lengthways and pass it through the machine on the thickest setting, folded end first. Repeat this step three times for each portion of dough.

Once laminated, pass each pasta sheet through the machine on each setting until you reach the second thinnest setting, using a little flour to prevent sticking. Lay the pasta out on the bench and cover with clean tea towels so it doesn't dry out while you make the filling.

Preheat the oven to 180°C (fan-forced). Cut the leeks in half lengthways, discarding the green tops and the outer leaves, then rinse under running water to remove any dirt. Pat dry with paper towel. Place on a baking tray dusted with semolina and bake for 15 minutes. Remove and sear in a hot chargrill pan until charred on all sides. Cool slightly, then roughly chop.

Pulse the leek, dill, breadcrumbs, egg, feta and half the chives in a food processor until combined.

Spoon tablespoons of filling onto one sheet of pasta, leaving a 2–3 cm gap between each one, then cut between each mound to form a square. Using a pastry brush, brush the egg yolk around the leek filling. Cut squares of the same size from the second sheet of pasta and gently lay over the top.

Place a 4 cm round cutter upside-down over the ravioli and gently press to remove all air bubbles (you need to make them tight so they don't explode). Seal the edges then cut them out with a 6 cm round cutter. Rest the ravioli in the fridge until needed – they'll be fine for up to 6 hours.

When you're ready to serve, cook the ravioli in boiling salted water for 5 minutes or until al dente. Drain and toss with the olive oil and extra feta then serve (five ravioli per person), garnished with the toasted almonds and remaining chives.

Serves 6

2 tablespoons extra virgin
  olive oil
1 brown onion, diced
3 cloves garlic, finely chopped
500 g minced beef
200 ml dry white wine
1 × 400 g tin crushed tomatoes
1 cinnamon stick
500 g dried macaroni pasta

Bechamel
1 litre full-cream milk
2 bay leaves
60 g unsalted butter
60 g plain flour
100 g feta, crumbled
1¼ cups (100 g) grated parmesan
¼ teaspoon cayenne pepper
1 teaspoon salt flakes
½ teaspoon cracked
  white pepper

Pasticcio

This is where the Italians got the idea for lasagne. Just joking! Pasticcio is a classic Hellenic pasta dish and I give it here in its traditional form – not a GC twist in sight. It's even better the next day.

Heat 1 tablespoon olive oil in a medium saucepan over medium heat. Add the onion and garlic and cook until softened, then add the minced beef and cook until browned, breaking up any lumps with a wooden spoon. Pour in the white wine and cook until reduced to a glaze, then add the crushed tomatoes and cinnamon stick and simmer for 20 minutes.

Meanwhile, cook the pasta in boiling salted water for 8–10 minutes until al dente. Drain and toss with the remaining olive oil. Set aside.

Preheat the oven to 180°C (fan-forced).

To make the bechamel, warm the milk in a medium saucepan with the bay leaves (don't let it boil). Turn off the heat and leave to infuse for 15 minutes. Remove the bay leaves.

Melt the butter in a separate saucepan, then add the flour and cook for 2 minutes, stirring constantly. Gradually add the milk and whisk over low heat until smooth, then simmer gently for a further 10 minutes or until cooked through. Remove from the heat and add the feta, parmesan, cayenne pepper, salt and pepper. Stir until melted and smooth.

To assemble, combine the beef mixture and pasta, then spoon into a greased deep baking dish. Pour over the bechamel sauce and bake for 15 minutes or until golden and bubbling.

Serves 4

100 ml extra virgin olive oil
1 clove garlic, thinly sliced
4 spring onions, thinly sliced
1 long red chilli, finely chopped
2 anchovy fillets in oil, drained
  on paper towel
1 teaspoon wholegrain mustard
40 g butter
45 ml white wine
200 g cooked spanner crab meat,
  shredded
2 teaspoons avgotaraho
  (cured cod roe)

Squid-ink hilopites pasta
1 teaspoon squid ink
1⅔ cups (250 g) type '00' flour,
  plus extra for dusting
½ teaspoon salt flakes
1 egg
3 large egg yolks
2 teaspoons extra virgin
  olive oil

Squid ink hilopites, Crab, avgotaraho

Avgotaraho is cured cod roe. It's the umami for the Greeks and you can find it at good fishmongers. The dish will still be delicious without it but do track it down if you can. Discovering new flavours and textures is what cooking is all about – it would be seriously boring if I just gave you on-trend recipes that are already in every magazine out there. Live a little!

To make the pasta dough, blend all the ingredients in a food processor until the mixture resembles fine breadcrumbs. Tip into a large bowl and knead for 2 minutes. Cover the bowl with plastic film and rest for 1 hour at room temperature.

Cut the dough in half and wrap one portion in plastic film. Pass the other portion of dough through a pasta machine on the thickest setting. To laminate the dough, fold it in half lengthways and pass it through the machine on the thickest setting, folded end first. Repeat this step three times for each portion of dough.

Once laminated, pass each pasta sheet through the machine on each setting until you reach the second thinnest setting, using a little flour to prevent sticking. Cut the pasta into 6 cm × 2 cm strips.

Cook the pasta in boiling salted water for 2–3 minutes or until al dente.

Meanwhile, heat the olive oil in a large frying pan over low heat, add the garlic and spring onion and saute gently until soft. Add the chilli, anchovies, mustard, butter and white wine and simmer for 1 minute.

Add the shredded crab and cooked pasta to the sauce and toss until the crab is warmed through. Serve garnished with avgotaraho.

Serves 4

350 g dried macaroni pasta
400 g fresh ricotta (see page 293)
80 g mizithra, grated or shaved
salt flakes and cracked pepper
extra virgin olive oil, for drizzling

Macaroni, ricotta, mizithra

This recipe was inspired by my good mate Massimo Bottura, who I consider to be Italy's best chef. As much as we love to argue about Greeks versus Italians, I will never forget the time we ate pasta together in Rome – a simple dish of spaghetti with pepper, butter and parmesan. This is my take on it, Greek style. Mizithra is a hard salty cheese that adds so much flavour here. Final tip: don't be afraid to finish with a really good grinding of pepper. It makes the dish.

Cook the pasta in boiling salted water for 4–5 minutes or until al dente. Drain, reserving some of the cooking water.

Loosen the ricotta with a little of the reserved cooking water, then toss through the pasta.

Serve topped with grated or shaved mizithra, salt and pepper and a good drizzle of olive oil.

Serves 4

1 × 1.4 kg chicken
4 litres chicken stock
　(see page 298)
2 eggs
juice of 2 lemons
salt flakes and cracked pepper
100 g feta, crumbled
oregano leaves, to garnish
2½ tablespoons extra virgin
　olive oil

Gnocchi
rock salt, for baking
400 g waxy potatoes, scrubbed
30 g cornflour
1½ tablespoons plain flour,
　plus extra if needed
2 egg yolks

Gnocchi avgolemono

Avgolemono is a classic egg and lemon soup that every Greek turns to when they feel under the weather. Suddenly you feel amazing! Combine that with soft, cloud-like gnocchi and you couldn't find a more comforting dish. The choice of potato is important for the gnocchi – it's best to use a waxy variety such as desiree or nicola.

Wash the chicken well in cold water, then place in a large saucepan with the chicken stock. Bring to the boil, then reduce the heat and simmer gently for 30 minutes or until cooked through. To check that it's cooked, pierce the skin on the inside of the leg – the liquid should run clear and the meat inside should be white.

Remove the chicken and set aside to cool. Skim the fat from the stock, then strain through a fine-meshed sieve into a clean saucepan. Bring the stock back to the boil, then reduce the heat and simmer until the liquid has reduced by half. Set aside until needed.

Strip all the meat off the chicken and shred by hand. Set aside.

Meanwhile, to make the gnocchi, preheat the oven to 180°C (fan-forced). Line a roasting tin with a layer of rock salt, add the potatoes and bake for 35 minutes or until soft. While still warm, peel off the skin and pass the potato through a potato ricer or sieve. Stir in the cornflour, plain flour and egg yolks, then gently knead until smooth, using extra flour if needed to stop the dough sticking to the bench. Take care not to overwork the dough. Roll the dough into long tubes approximately 1 cm in diameter and cut into 1 cm lengths.

Cook the gnocchi in boiling salted water for 1–2 minutes or until they rise to the surface. As soon as they do, scoop them out with a slotted spoon and refresh in a bowl of iced water.

Bring the reduced chicken stock to the boil. Remove from the heat, add the eggs and blitz with a stick blender until smooth. Add the shredded chicken and gnocchi and gently heat through. Stir in the lemon juice and season to taste with salt and pepper.

Divide among bowls and garnish with the feta and oregano leaves. Finish with a drizzle of olive oil and a final grinding of pepper.

Serves 4

1 bunch curly parsley
20 g unsalted butter
1 spring onion, thinly sliced
1 clove garlic, thinly sliced
½ cup (125 ml) thickened cream
1 litre chicken stock
   (see page 298)
⅓ cup (80 ml) extra virgin olive oil

1 brown onion, finely diced
1½ cups (300 g) carnaroli rice
500 g baby spinach
1 cup (80 g) finely grated
   kefalograviera cheese
finely grated zest and juice
   of 1 lemon
salt flakes and cracked pepper

Spanakoriso

This is a classic dish, full of iron and carbs – great for anyone preparing for a sports event. The key here is to keep the mixture loose, rather than stiff or dry. I wouldn't normally choose curly parsley but it's a must for this dish as it holds up in flavour and colour. Kefalograviera is a hard sheep and goat's milk cheese. If you can't get your hands on it you can use good-quality parmesan.

Bring 2 litres water to the boil in a large saucepan. Pick the leaves from the parsley and blanch until soft (the parsley must be soft enough to puree). Drain and refresh in cold water.

Melt the butter in a small saucepan over low heat and gently cook the spring onion and garlic until softened. Pour in the cream and bring to the boil.

While the cream is coming to the boil, drain the parsley and squeeze out any excess liquid. Remove the cream from the heat. Add the parsley and blend with a stick blender until completely smooth. Keep refrigerated until needed.

Bring the chicken stock to a simmer and keep it hot.

Heat ¼ cup (60 ml) olive oil in a medium saucepan over medium heat, add the onion and cook until softened. Increase the heat to high, add the rice and stir constantly for 2 minutes to ensure the grains of rice are well coated. Reduce the heat to medium, add 1 cup (250 ml) hot stock and stir until completely absorbed. Add the remaining stock and bring to the boil. Cover with a lid, reduce the heat to as low as possible and simmer for 10 minutes. Turn off the heat and set the rice aside, still covered.

Heat the remaining olive oil in a large frying pan and saute the spinach until wilted. Transfer the spinach to a chopping board and roughly chop, then add to the rice with the parsley puree, kefalograviera, lemon zest and juice. Stir well and season to taste, then serve.

Prawn saganaki tortellini,
tomato and mustard-seed vinaigrette
(see page 90)

Serves 4

200 g raw prawns, peeled
  and deveined
2 egg whites
¼ cup (60 ml) pure cream
  (35% fat)
2–3 tablespoons roughly
  chopped dill
salt flakes
cayenne pepper, to taste
2 egg yolks, lightly beaten
crumbled feta, for sprinkling
roughly chopped chervil and dill,
  to garnish

Tortellini pasta

2⅔ cups (400 g) type '00' flour,
  plus extra for dusting
4 eggs
2 teaspoons extra virgin olive oil
1 teaspoon salt flakes

**Tomato and mustard-seed
  vinaigrette**

2 cloves garlic
200 g cherry tomatoes, cut in half
1 cup (250 ml) extra virgin olive oil
2 golden shallots, thinly sliced
½ teaspoon yellow mustard seeds
½ teaspoon black mustard seeds
⅓ cup (80 ml) chardonnay vinegar
  (or any good white wine vinegar)
2 anchovy fillets in oil, drained
  on paper towel
2 tablespoons roughly chopped
  flat-leaf parsley
2 tablespoons roughly
  chopped dill
salt flakes and cracked pepper

Prawn Saganaki tortellini, tomato and mustard-seed vinaigrette

Pictured
Page 89

Blend the prawn meat and egg whites in a food processor until very smooth (try to keep the mixture as cold as possible). Remove from the processor and gently stir in the cream and dill. Season to taste with salt and cayenne pepper, then keep in the fridge until needed

To make the pasta dough, blend all the ingredients in a food processor until the mixture resembles fine breadcrumbs. Tip into a large bowl and knead for 2 minutes. Cover the bowl with plastic film and rest for 1 hour at room temperature.

Cut the dough in half and wrap one portion in plastic film. Pass the other portion of dough through a pasta machine on the thickest setting. To laminate the dough, fold it in half lengthways and pass it through the machine on the thickest setting, folded end first. Repeat this step three times for each portion of dough.

Once laminated, pass each pasta sheet through the machine on each setting until you reach the second thinnest setting, using a little flour to prevent sticking. Lay the pasta out on the bench and cut into 8 cm squares.

Place 1 tablespoon of the prawn filling in the centre of each square, then cut out with a 6 cm round cutter. Using a pastry brush, brush the edges with a little egg yolk, then fold over to encase the filling. Press gently with your fingers to remove any air pockets. Bring the two points of each piece of pasta together to form tortellini. Place on a well-floured tray and store in the fridge, uncovered, until needed.

To make the vinaigrette, preheat the oven to 170°C (fan-forced) and line a baking tray with baking paper. Wrap the garlic cloves in foil and place on the prepared tray with the cherry tomatoes. Bake for 10 minutes or until softened. Remove and roughly crush the garlic cloves with the back of a heavy knife.

Meanwhile, heat the olive oil in a large saucepan over low heat and saute the shallot until golden brown. Add the mustard seeds and cook until they pop. Add the vinegar, anchovies, cherry tomatoes and garlic and stir until the anchovies have melted into the oil. Add the chopped herbs and season to taste with salt and pepper. Keep warm while you cook the pasta.

Cook the tortellini in boiling salted water for 4 minutes or until al dente. Remove with a slotted spoon and toss through the warm vinaigrette. Divide among serving bowls and top with crumbled feta and herbs.

This is my play on the classic baked prawns with feta saganaki dish, and is one of my all-time favourites. You want to be cooking this during tomato season as it's the tomato vinaigrette that brings it all together. Don't be afraid of the prawn mousse: use large, fleshy prawns and keep the mixture as cool as possible so the proteins stay together.

Serves 4

200 ml extra virgin olive oil
8 golden shallots, thinly sliced
4 cloves garlic, thinly sliced
120 g white anchovies
6 vine-ripened tomatoes
500 g spaghetti
large handful of flat-leaf parsley,
  roughly chopped
finely grated zest of 1 lemon

Garlic breadcrumbs
80 g butter
2 tablespoons extra virgin olive oil
2 cloves garlic, finely chopped
½ cup (35 g) fresh breadcrumbs
salt flakes

Spaghetti, anchovies, parsley, garlic breadcrumbs

This simple pasta dish pays homage to my Italian grandmother and her Sicilian heart. The fresh tomato seeds are what it's all about here – this is where all the flavour comes from. If you can't find white anchovies its okay to use normal Spanish or Italian ones.

Heat the olive oil in a frying pan over medium heat, add the shallot and cook gently until translucent. Add the garlic and anchovies and cook for 2 minutes or until the anchovies have melted into the oil. Squeeze out the pulp from the tomatoes and toss it through the mixture, then let the tomato cook down for 3–4 minutes.

Cook the spaghetti in boiling salted water for 3–5 minutes or until al dente.

Meanwhile, to make the garlic breadcrumbs, heat the butter and olive oil in a frying pan until the butter has melted. Add the garlic and breadcrumbs and toss until golden and crunchy. Season with salt.

Drain the spaghetti and add it directly to the sauce, tossing well to combine. Add the parsley and toss again. Sprinkle with the lemon zest and garlic breadcrumbs and serve immediately.

A HEATED EXCHANGE AND A LESSON LEARNED

I spent an incredible few days with Antonio Carluccio on a boat from Amsterdam to Budapest raising money for a good friend of ours, Matt Golinski. It was an amazing experience but the real wealth was the memories we created. For example, one afternoon I became Antonio's commis chef and we made risotto together. I was about to pour wine into the risotto because that's what we always do, but very quickly learnt this is a big no-no in Antonio's eyes. He became very animated and upset at me; and through this heated exchange he taught me that just because every other chef puts wine in their risotto it doesn't mean I have to. I loved that he was so passionate about something so basic. The lesson here is simple: to be a great cook you have to be concerned about the details. It's not about the big picture – it's about all the little things done well.

For me this means it's not about learning to cook – it's about loving life.

Love it and respect it. Strong beliefs and loving what you do are the keys to success.

Risotto of mushroom 'Antonio Carluccio'

Serves 4

2 cloves garlic, unpeeled
25 g dried porcini mushrooms,
    soaked in hot water
400 g mixed wild mushrooms,
    wiped clean and torn into
    bite-sized pieces
60 g unsalted butter
4 sprigs thyme, leaves picked
¼ teaspoon salt flakes
⅛ teaspoon freshly ground
    white pepper
grated parmesan and extra
    virgin olive oil, to serve

Risotto
1.5 litres chicken stock
    (see page 298)
2 tablespoons extra virgin
    olive oil
110 g unsalted butter
½ white onion, finely diced
1¾ cups (350 g) carnaroli rice
60 g parmesan, finely grated
½ teaspoon salt flakes
¼ teaspoon freshly ground
    white pepper

To make the risotto, pour the stock into a large saucepan and bring to a simmer.

Meanwhile, heat the olive oil and 60 g butter in a large heavy-based saucepan over medium–low heat, add the onion and cook until translucent. Add the rice and mix well to coat all the grains. Add the stock, a few ladles at a time, and cook over medium heat, stirring frequently until each addition of stock has been absorbed. Don't let the rice dry out. When you have added most of the stock test the rice to ensure it is al dente. Add a little more stock, along with the parmesan and remaining butter and beat until smooth. Season with salt and pepper, then cover with a clean tea towel and then a lid and leave to rest for 1–2 minutes.

While the risotto is cooking, preheat the oven to 180°C (fan-forced). Wrap the garlic cloves in foil and roast for 7 minutes. Allow to cool, then remove the skins and crush the garlic.

Strain the liquid from the dried porcini. Add the wild and porcini mushrooms to the risotto and cook for a few minutes. Add the butter, garlic and thyme and lightly toss to combine. Season to taste with salt and pepper.

Spoon the risotto onto plates, allowing it to ooze and spread. Top with freshly grated parmesan and a drizzle of extra virgin olive oil and serve.

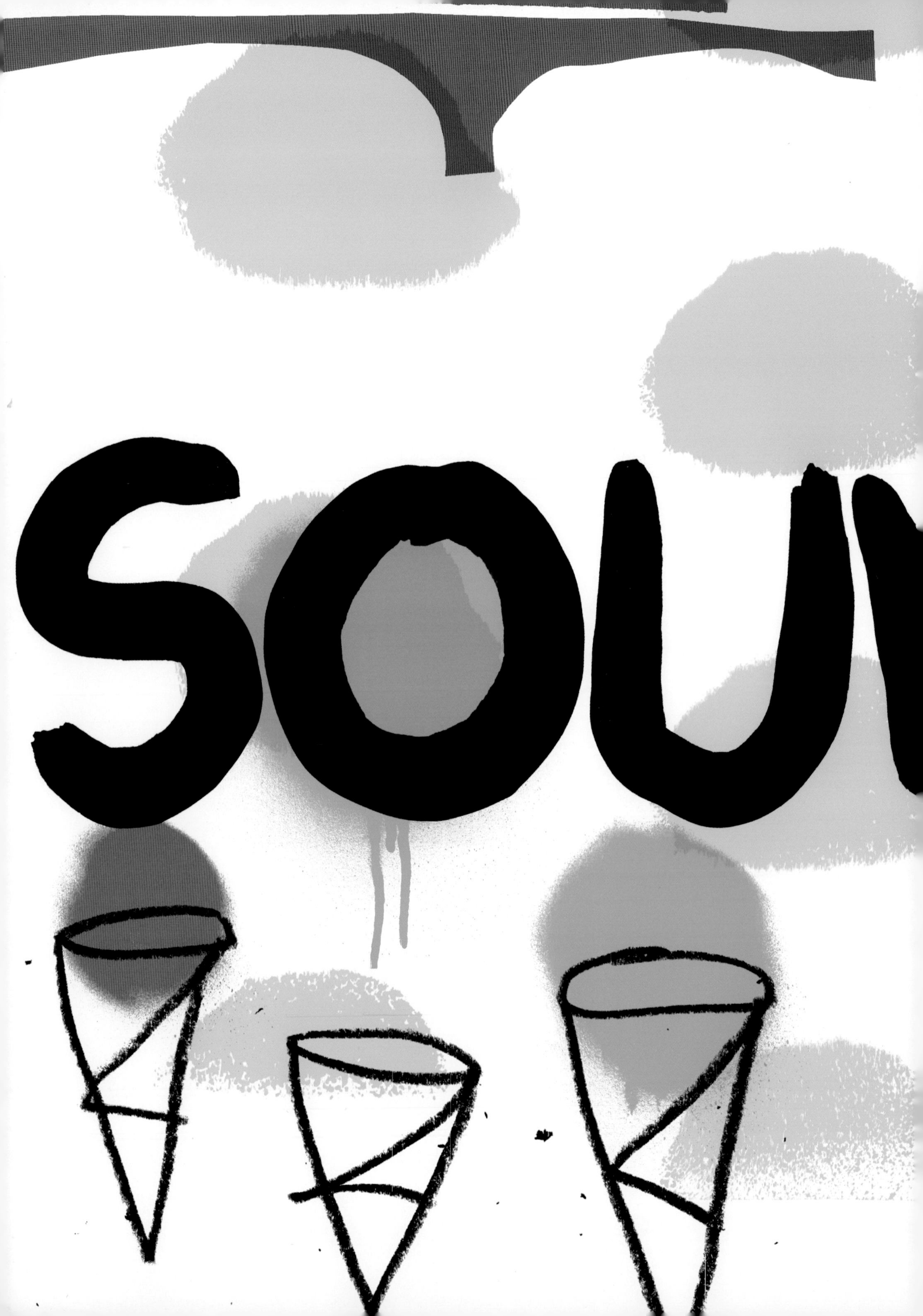
SOU

THE SEVEN SOUVLAKI COMMANDMENTS

1. A KEBAB IS NOT A SOUVLAKI

2. MY SOUVAS ARE NOT MADE AFTER 11 PM

3. ANYTHING CAN GO IN A SOUVLAKI — BUT ONLY IF IT IS GOOD QUALITY

4. A SOUVLAKI IS NOT A MEAL; IT IS A SOCIAL PART OF LIFE

5. GYROS MEANS TO TURN. IT'S NOT A SOUVLAKI

6. MEAT ON A STICK IS A KALAMAKI, NOT A SOUVLAKI

7. THE SOUVLAKI THAT IS EATEN MOST OFTEN AROUND THE WORLD IS MADE WITH PORK. GREEKS DON'T EAT LAMB MUCH.

Souvlaki — 101

Serves 4

4 small pita breads (see page 289)
extra virgin olive oil, for brushing

Pork sheftalia
1 clove garlic, unpeeled
400 g minced pork
½ small red onion, finely diced
finely grated zest of 2 oranges
2 teaspoons fennel seeds,
   toasted and crushed

Coriander tabouli
1 heaped tablespoon burghul
salt flakes
large handful of coriander leaves
finely grated zest of 1 lemon
1¼ tablespoons lemon juice
1¼ tablespoons extra virgin
   olive oil
½ teaspoon ground sumac
cracked pepper

Tahini yoghurt
2½ tablespoons natural
   Greek-style yoghurt
2–3 teaspoons tahini
3 teaspoons lemon juice
¼ teaspoon salt flakes
2 teaspoons extra virgin olive oil

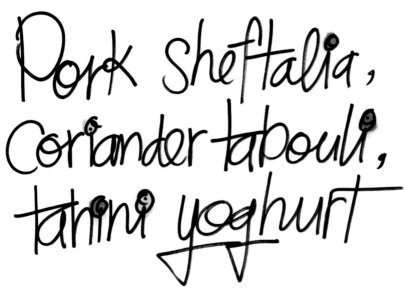

Pork sheftalia,
Coriander tabouli,
tahini yoghurt

For me, a well-made souvlaki is a wonderful thing – not something to be wolfed down at 3 o'clock in the morning. It should be delicate, refined and delicious. I remember the first time I ate this particular combination. I was sitting on a tacky plastic chair in Cyprus, enjoying an ice-cold beer and absolutely smashing one of these souvlaki.

To make the pork sheftalia, preheat the oven to 180°C (fan-forced). Wrap the garlic clove in foil and roast for 10–15 minutes or until soft. Allow to cool, then remove the skin and finely chop. Combine with the pork, onion, orange zest and fennel seeds in a large bowl and mix well by hand for 5 minutes or until sticky. Divide the mixture into 12 portions and form into sausages. Place on a lined baking tray and rest in the fridge for 1 hour before using.

To make the coriander tabouli, place the burghul in a small saucepan with 1 cup (250 ml) water and a pinch of salt and bring to the boil. Reduce the heat and simmer gently for 15 minutes or until tender. Drain and set aside to cool. Combine the burghul and coriander in a bowl. Whisk together the lemon zest and juice, olive oil, sumac and 1 teaspoon water and season with salt and pepper. Toss the dressing through the burghul and coriander.

To prepare the tahini yoghurt, combine all the ingredients in a small bowl.

Preheat a barbecue grill plate or heavy-based non-stick frying pan over high heat. Cook the sheftalia for 3 minutes each side or until cooked through, then remove and rest for 2 minutes.

Brush the pita breads with olive oil and grill lightly on both sides.

Spoon 1 tablespoon tahini yoghurt onto each pita bread, then top with tabouli and three sheftalia. Roll up and serve.

Zucchini keftedes,
burghul salad (see page 106)

Serves 4

2 zucchini (courgettes)
salt flakes
1 clove garlic, unpeeled
2–3 tablespoons roughly
  chopped mint
1 egg
1½ tablespoons cornflour
1 teaspoon fennel seeds,
  toasted and crushed
2–3 tablespoons roughly
  chopped flat-leaf parsley
cracked pepper
vegetable oil, for deep-frying
4 small pita bread (see page 289)
extra virgin olive oil, for brushing

Burghul salad
½ cup (80 g) burghul
salt flakes
large handful of flat-leaf parsley
  leaves, roughly chopped
1 small red onion, finely diced
finely grated zest and juice
  of 1 lemon
1 tablespoon extra virgin olive oil
cracked pepper

Zucchini keftedes, burghul salad

This vegetarian souvlaki is
a nice way to eat from the
middle of the table. Lay out
all the components separately
and let everyone make their
own. Any leftover salad makes
a great lunch the next day.

Grate the zucchini into a bowl. Season with ½ teaspoon salt and set
aside for 1 hour, then place in the centre of a clean J-cloth or square
of muslin and wring out any excess moisture.

Meanwhile, preheat the oven to 180°C (fan-forced). Wrap the garlic
clove in foil and roast for 10–15 minutes or until soft. Allow to cool,
then remove the skin and crush the garlic.

Combine the zucchini, garlic, mint, egg, cornflour, fennel seeds, parsley,
salt and pepper in a large bowl and mix very well by hand. Form the
mixture into bite-sized balls, then place on a lined baking tray and rest
in the fridge until needed.

To make the burghul salad, place the burghul in a small saucepan with
plenty of water and a pinch of salt and bring to the boil. Reduce the heat
and simmer gently for 15 minutes or until tender. Drain and set aside to
cool. Combine the burghul, parsley, onion, lemon zest and juice in
a bowl. Add the olive oil and season to taste with salt and pepper.

Heat the oil for deep-frying in a deep-fryer to 180°C (or in a heavy-based
saucepan until a cube of bread browns in 15 seconds). Add the zucchini
keftedes in batches and cook for 7–8 minutes or until golden brown.
Remove with a slotted spoon and drain on paper towel. Season lightly
with salt flakes.

Brush the pita breads with olive oil and grill lightly on both sides.

Spoon the salad onto each pita bread, then top with the keftedes.
Roll up and serve.

Pictured
page 105

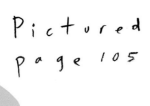

Serves 4

1 clove garlic, unpeeled
4 baby turnips
100 g peas (preferably fresh),
  blanched
2–3 tablespoons roughly
  chopped mint
80 g fresh ricotta (see page 293)
salt flakes and cracked pepper

200 g lamb sweetbreads,
  membrane removed (ask your
  butcher to do this for you)
1½ tablespoons vegetable oil
4 small pita breads (see page 289)
extra virgin olive oil, for brushing
⅓ cup (80 g) cauliflower skordalia
  (see page 46)

Crispy sweetbreads, peas, mint, ricotta

Pictured page 109

I fed my best mate Steve Messina sweetbreads recently. He was pretty reluctant to try them but of course once he did he devoured them. Now I love Steve dearly but he is a tinned fish and rice type of guy, so if *he* can eat sweetbreads then so can you. The key here is to get to know your butcher and find out when they have fresh sweetbreads available for you to buy.

Preheat the oven to 180°C (fan-forced). Wrap the garlic clove in foil and roast for 10–15 minutes or until soft. Allow to cool, then remove the skin and crush the garlic.

Wash and dry the turnips, then slice very thinly using a mandolin.

Combine the garlic, turnip, peas, mint and ricotta in a bowl. Season with salt and pepper, then cover and keep in the fridge until needed.

Pat the lamb sweetbreads dry with paper towel.

Heat the vegetable oil in a frying pan over medium heat, add the sweetbreads and cook for 7–10 minutes or until golden on all sides. Remove from the pan and rest on a plate lined with paper towel. Season with salt flakes.

Brush the pita breads with olive oil and grill lightly on both sides.

Spoon the cauliflower skordalia, pea and ricotta mixture and sweetbreads onto each pita bread. Roll up and serve.

Crispy sweetbreads, peas, mint, ricotta
(see page 107)

Serves 4

4 large banana prawns, peeled
  and deveined
1 clove garlic, crushed
2½ tablespoons extra virgin
  olive oil
8 cherry tomatoes, cut in half
2 golden shallots, thinly sliced
12 kalamata olives, pitted
1 tablespoon salted baby capers,
  rinsed and roughly chopped
1 tablespoon roughly chopped
  flat-leaf parsley

juice of ½ lemon
salt flakes and cracked pepper
4 small pita breads (see page 289)
extra virgin olive oil, extra,
  for brushing
⅓ cup (80 g) white bean skordalia
  (see page 58)
50 g thinly sliced jamon

Grilled prawns, Jamon, tomato, Capers

Not your classic souvlaki
but again I'm having fun
with it, and I've always loved
the combination of jamon
and prawns. Remember,
a souvlaki is meant to be
made fresh and eaten straight
away. Don't let it sit around –
eat, my friends, eat.

Combine the prawns, garlic and 1 tablespoon olive oil in a non-reactive
bowl and set aside to marinate for a few minutes.

Mix together the cherry tomatoes, shallot, olives, capers, parsley,
lemon juice and remaining olive oil and season with salt and pepper.

Heat a chargrill pan or barbecue grill or flatplate until hot and grill
the prawns until cooked through.

Brush the pita breads with extra olive oil and grill lightly on both sides.

Spoon the white bean skordalia and tomato salad onto each pita bread,
then top with the prawns and jamon. Roll up and serve.

Serves 4

2½ tablespoons cornflour
3 teaspoons ground coriander
½ head cauliflower, cut into
small florets
vegetable oil, for deep-frying
salt flakes and cracked pepper
300 g boneless chicken thighs,
skin on, trimmed

⅓ cup (100 g) mayonnaise
(see page 292)
4 small pita breads (see page 289)
extra virgin olive oil, for brushing
⅓ cup (80 g) peanut and
coriander-seed hummus
(see page 51)

Roast chicken, fried Cauliflower, hummus

Chicken, cauliflower and hummus: nothing tricky, just simple flavours that work so well together. Make sure you have all the ingredients ready to go before you start rolling, or put everything on the table and make it communal activity. A dining experience is just as much about the company as it is about the food and drinks.

Preheat the oven to 200°C (fan-forced) and line a baking tray with baking paper.

Combine the cornflour and coriander in a bowl, add the cauliflower florets and toss to coat, shaking off any excess.

Heat the oil for deep-frying in a deep-fryer to 180°C (or in a heavy-based saucepan until a cube of bread browns in 15 seconds). Add the cauliflower in batches and cook until golden. Remove with a slotted spoon and drain on paper towel, then season with salt and pepper.

Coat the chicken in the cornflour mixture, then place on the prepared tray and roast for 15 minutes. Season with salt and set aside.

Cut the chicken into 1 cm thick slices and place in a bowl with the cauliflower. Add the mayonnaise and mix until well coated.

Brush the pita breads with extra olive oil and grill lightly on both sides.

Spoon the hummus onto each pita bread, then top with the chicken and cauliflower mixture. Roll up and serve.

Serves 4

300 g piece boneless
  lamb shoulder
salt flakes and cracked pepper
150 ml extra virgin olive oil
½ small brown onion, diced
½ baby leek, white part only,
  diced
2 cloves garlic, finely diced
200 ml white wine
200 ml chicken stock
  (see page 298)

3 sprigs thyme
3 star anise
4 small pita breads (see page 289)
extra virgin olive oil, extra,
  for brushing
120 g miso melitzanosalata
  (see page 52)
mint leaves, to garnish

Slow-cooked lamb, miso eggplant

The Greeks stole eggplant from the Turks and now I'm stealing miso from the Japanese. I love this combination. The miso gives the eggplant a really meaty flavour – don't be afraid to add a little more to suit your taste.

Preheat the oven to 120°C (fan-forced).

Season the lamb shoulder with salt and pepper. Heat the olive oil in a flameproof casserole dish over medium heat and sear the lamb until golden brown all over. Remove to a plate. Add the onion, leek and garlic and cook until translucent. Deglaze with the white wine and let it simmer until reduced by half, then add the chicken stock, thyme sprigs and star anise. Return the lamb to the casserole and season with salt and pepper.

Cover securely with a lid, then transfer to the oven and cook gently for 2–2½ hours or until tender.

Remove the casserole from the oven and set aside to cool. Once cool, remove the lamb. Strain the stock through a fine sieve and reserve for another use, such as a sauce or risotto. Cut the lamb into bite-sized pieces.

Brush the pita breads with olive oil and grill lightly on both sides.

Spoon 1 tablespoon eggplant dip onto each pita bread and top with the lamb. Garnish with mint leaves, then roll up and serve.

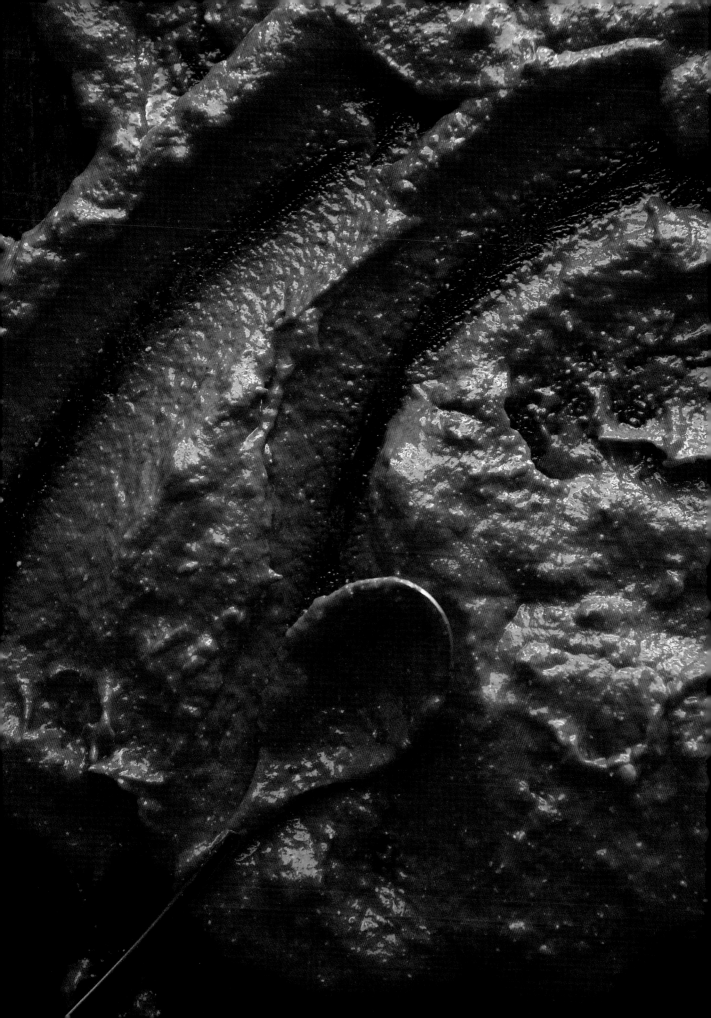

Serves 4

2 tablespoons salt flakes
1 tablespoon fennel seeds
1 tablespoon coriander seeds
1.4 kg boneless pork belly
½ cup (150 g) rock salt
4 large pita breads (see page 289)
extra virgin olive oil, for brushing

Tirokafteri
4 red capsicums (peppers)
1 long red chilli
1 teaspoon salt flakes
1 teaspoon aleppo flakes
100 g feta

Toursi
½ head cauliflower, cut into
  2 cm florets
1 carrot, cut in half, then cut
  into 2 cm × 1 cm pieces
1 stick celery, cut into 2 cm ×
  1 cm pieces
2 cups (500 ml) white wine
  vinegar
1 tablespoon salt flakes
1 tablespoon caster sugar
10 peppercorns
1 star anise
8 coriander seeds

Roast pork, toursi, tirokafteri

Pictured page 120

Combine the salt, fennel and coriander seeds and sprinkle over the pork. Leave to cure, uncovered, for 4 hours or overnight in the fridge.

Meanwhile, to make the tirokafteri, preheat the oven to 190°C (fan-forced). Place the capsicums on a baking tray and bake for 20 minutes, turning once. Transfer them to a bowl, cover with plastic film and leave to cool for 15 minutes. Peel the capsicums and remove the seeds, then place in a colander to drain for a couple of hours to remove the excess liquid. Place the drained capsicums in a blender with the remaining ingredients and blend until smooth. Store in the fridge until needed.

Preheat the oven to 200°C (fan-forced).

Using a sharp knife, score the skin of the pork belly to a depth of 1 cm. Place the belly in a colander in the sink and pour over 2–3 litres boiling water to scald the skin. Pat dry.

Place the belly on a rack inside a roasting tin, skin-side up, and rub with the rock salt. Transfer to the oven and roast for 40–50 minutes or until the skin is well blistered. Reduce the temperature to 120°C (fan-forced) and cook for a further 1 hour 25 minutes or until tender and the juices run clear when pierced with a knife. Set aside to rest for 15 minutes, then cut into 5 mm thick slices.

To make the toursi, place the cauliflower, carrot and celery in a sterilised jar with a sealable lid (see Note). Combine the vinegar, salt, sugar, peppercorns, star anise, coriander seeds and 2 cups (500 ml) water in a medium saucepan and bring to a simmer. Pour the pickling liquid over the vegetables, leaving a 1 cm gap below the rim. Seal with the lid.

Place the jar in a clean saucepan and pour in enough water to come halfway up the side of the jar. Simmer for 10 minutes. Set aside to cool, then store in the fridge until needed.

Brush the pita breads with olive oil and grill lightly on both sides.

Spoon the tirokafteri onto each pita bread, then top with the toursi and roasted pork. Roll up tightly using baking paper to hold the souvlaki.

Everyone thinks Greeks eat lamb all the time. WRONG! In Greece they eat lamb for Easter celebrations, and it's young baby lamb. Throughout the year they eat pork and can I tell you it's delicious. Toursi, which are basically Greek pickles, make a great refreshing point for the dish.

Sterilising jars
To sterilise a jar, fill the jar with boiling water from the kettle, then tip the water out and leave the jar to dry. Make sure you sterilise the lid too.

Roast pork, toursi, tirokafteri
(see page 118)

Beef short rib, bone marrow, red onion salad, horseradish tzatziki (see page 122)

Serves 4

1 tablespoon extra virgin olive oil
400 g boneless beef short rib
1 brown onion, peeled
    and cut into wedges
4 cloves garlic, finely chopped
3 sprigs thyme
1 cinnamon stick
100 ml red wine
100 ml port
400 ml beef stock
100 g bone marrow
    (see introduction)
4 small pita breads (see page 289)
extra virgin olive oil, for brushing

Horseradish tzatziki

1 Lebanese cucumber
salt flakes
100 g natural Greek-style yoghurt
2 teaspoons horseradish cream
finely grated zest and juice
    of ½ lemon
2–3 tablespoons shredded mint
2–3 tablespoons roughly
    chopped dill
cracked pepper

Red onion salad

1 red onion, very thinly sliced
    (preferably with a mandolin)
large handful of flat-leaf
    parsley leaves
1 tablespoon extra virgin olive oil
finely grated zest and juice
    of 1 lemon

Pictured
Page 121

Beef short rib, bone marrow, red onion salad, horseradish tzatziki

Preheat the oven to 120°C (fan-forced).

Heat the olive oil in a flameproof casserole dish over medium–high heat and sear the beef until golden brown. Remove and set aside.

Add the onion, garlic, thyme and cinnamon stick to the pan and saute until the onion is golden brown. Return the beef to the pan. Deglaze with the red wine and let it simmer until almost dry, then repeat with the port. Add the stock, then cover and transfer to the oven to gently braise for 3½–4 hours or until tender.

Remove the beef and strain the stock through a fine sieve into a clean saucepan. Heat the stock and simmer until reduced by half. Cut the beef into eight pieces (making sure there are no bones) and return to the sauce. Set aside until needed, or refrigerate if you are making it ahead of time.

Cut the bone marrow into 1 cm thick pieces and soak in iced water to remove any traces of blood.

For the horseradish tzatziki, cut the cucumber in half lengthways and remove the seeds with a spoon, then grate into a small colander. Mix with 2 tablespoons salt and set aside for 2 hours, then place in the centre of a clean J-cloth or square of muslin and wring out any excess moisture. Combine the cucumber, yoghurt, horseradish cream, lemon zest and juice, mint and dill, and season to taste with pepper.

To make the red onion salad, combine the onion and parsley in a bowl. Add the olive oil, lemon zest and juice and toss to coat.

Just before serving, add the bone marrow to the beef and gently reheat.

Brush the pita breads with olive oil and grill lightly on both sides.

Spoon the horseradish tzatziki onto each pita bread, then top with the braised beef rib, marrow and onion salad. Roll up and serve.

Get to know your butcher, and when he has fresh bone marrow make sure you buy some. It will add a lovely texture and richness to your souvlaki. Try to get your hands on horseradish cream made with fresh horseradish (or make your own) – most of the time the stuff that comes in a jar is wasabi. Life is too short to eat bad food.

Soft-shell crab, fresh herbs,
honey, mayonnaise
(see page 126)

Serves 4

large handful of coriander sprigs
large handful of mint sprigs
125 g honey
juice of 1 lime
1 tablespoon fish sauce
⅔ cup (130 g) tapioca flour
⅔ cup (130 g) rice flour
2 teaspoons aleppo flakes

4 soft-shell crabs
vegetable oil, for deep-frying
salt flakes
4 large pita breads (see page 289)
extra virgin olive oil, for brushing
120 g Japanese mayonnaise
2 tablespoons flaked almonds,
    toasted

Pictured page 125

Soft-Shell Crab, fresh herbs, honey, mayonnaise

This is one of our biggest sellers at Gazi. I love it as it not only represents modern Greece, it also represents who I am: an adventurous chef with an Australian heart and a Greek state of mind.

Wash the coriander and mint well in iced water. Pick off the leaves and discard the stalks.

In a small saucepan, bring the honey and lime juice to a simmer, add the fish sauce, then set aside to cool.

Combine the tapioca flour, rice flour and aleppo flakes in a shallow bowl.

Cut the crabs in half and clean under running water, then pat dry with paper towel. Add to the flour mixture and toss gently to coat, shaking off any excess.

Heat the oil for deep-frying in a deep-fryer to 180°C (or in a heavy-based saucepan until a cube of bread browns in 15 seconds). Add the crab pieces in batches and cook for 3–4 minutes or until crunchy and cooked through. Remove with a slotted spoon and drain on paper towel. Season with salt flakes.

Brush the pita breads with olive oil and grill lightly on both sides.

Spoon the mayonnaise onto each pita bread, then top with the fried crab and fresh herbs. Drizzle with the honey sauce and sprinkle with flaked almonds. Roll up tightly using baking paper to hold the souvlaki.

Serves 4

4 duck legs
250 g rock salt
1 tablespoon coriander seeds
1 tablespoon fennel seeds
1.25 kg duck fat
150 g caster sugar
1 star anise
1 pear
⅓ cup (65 g) rice flour
⅓ cup (65 g) tapioca flour

1 tablespoon aleppo flakes
vegetable oil, for deep-frying
4 large pita breads (see page 289)
extra virgin olive oil, for brushing
⅓ cup (100 g) mayonnaise
    (see page 292)
1 red onion, very thinly sliced
    (preferably with a mandolin)
2 large handfuls of flat-leaf
    parsley, leaves picked

Crispy duck, Poached pear, mayonnaise

First up, you'll need to start this recipe a day in advance to get the duck cooked properly. The combination of pear and duck is pretty spectacular, but this is about texture too. Make sure the duck is good and crispy before you assemble the souvlaki.

Pictured
Page 129

Place the duck legs on a baking tray and rub with rock salt, coriander and fennel seeds. Cure in the fridge for at least 8 hours, or overnight.

Preheat the oven to 75°C (fan-forced).

Rinse the duck and pat dry with paper towel. Place the legs and duck fat in a deep baking dish and cook them in the oven overnight for 12 hours.

The following day, when the duck fat is cool enough to handle, carefully remove the meat from the bone, keeping the meat pieces as large as possible. Set aside in the fridge.

Place the sugar, star anise and 1 litre water in a medium saucepan and bring to simmer until the sugar has dissolved. Peel and core the pear (if liked), then place in the syrup and cover with a cartouche (a round of baking paper). Poach for 20–25 minutes or until soft and the tip of a knife can easily be inserted into the pear. Set the pan aside and allow the pear to cool in the liquid, then remove and cut the pear into thin slices. Return the syrup to the heat and simmer until reduced by half.

Combine the tapioca flour, rice flour and aleppo flakes in a shallow bowl. Add the duck meat and toss gently to coat, shaking off any excess.

Heat the oil for deep-frying in a deep-fryer to 180°C (or in a heavy-based saucepan until a cube of bread browns in 15 seconds). Add the duck pieces in batches and cook for 1–2 minutes or until golden. Remove with a slotted spoon and drain on paper towel.

Brush the pita breads with olive oil and grill lightly on both sides.

Spoon the mayonnaise onto each pita bread, then top with the pear, red onion, parsley and chucks of confit duck. Finish with a drizzle of pear syrup. Roll up tightly using baking paper to hold the souvlaki.

Crispy duck, poached pear,
mayonnaise (see page 127)

RESPECTING THE MAN, RESPECTING THE CHEF

I am lucky to work in an industry that allows you to meet so many wonderful people. Over the years Marco Pierre White has become a great friend and supporter of mine. I respect and look up to him, not just for his cooking ability but also for his outlook on life and what we do as cooks.

I remember the day after a review for my new Press Club was published. It was not good at all – more of a character assassination rather than a review on food, service and all the things that make a restaurant. When I arrived at the MasterChef set I was so upset, crying like a big baby. I will never forget what Marco said: 'George, at the end of the day is it all worth it, to be judged by people with less knowledge than us?' I can't tell you how much it helped.

Through this dish I pay my respects to Marco and acknowledge his impact on my life. His book *White Heat* was my first ever cookbook – I bought it when I was an apprentice and to this day I still read it and love it.

MPW: 'Mother Nature is the true artist.'

GDC: 'So true Marco. We are so blessed that Mother Nature gives us every opportunity to succeed, and we are the only ones to destroy it.'

Confit Salmon, tomato butter sauce

Serves 4

800 g piece salmon fillet,
  skin and bones removed
salt flakes

Confit oil
1 litre extra virgin olive oil
2 cloves garlic, skin on, crushed
2 star anise
10 juniper berries
5 sprigs thyme
10 white peppercorns
2 bay leaves
2 teaspoons fennel seeds
finely grated zest of 1 lemon

Tomato butter sauce
20 cherry tomatoes
⅓ cup (80 ml) tomato ketchup
160 g chilled butter, cut into
  small dice
pinch of freshly ground
  white pepper

To make the confit oil, place all the ingredients in a saucepan and cook at 95°C for 1 hour (use a cooking thermometer to maintain the correct temperature). Remove from the heat and cool completely.

Heat the oil to 60°C, add the salmon fillet and heat gently until the core temperature of the fish is 40°C (this will take about 20–25 minutes).

Meanwhile, to make the tomato butter sauce, blitz the tomatoes and tomato ketchup in a blender or with a stick blender. Pass through a fine sieve and gently bring to the boil in a small saucepan. Reduce the heat and whisk the cold butter into the sauce until melted, adding one or two chunks at a time. (You can increase the quantity of butter in each addition once the sauce has started to emulsify.) Season with white pepper, then keep the sauce warm (but under 88°C or else it will split).

Season the salmon with salt and serve immediately with the tomato butter sauce.

Serves 4

6 sebago potatoes
salt flakes
vegetable oil, for deep-frying
8 cloves garlic, unpeeled
100 ml extra virgin olive oil
100 g feta, crumbled
½ teaspoon dried oregano

Patates tiganites, feta, roast garlic oil

Chips with feta. I was recently told by a customer in my restaurant that she could not believe I would serve such a dish; apparently she didn't consider it representative of a GC dish. I suppose everyone is entitled to their opinion but at the end of the day it's just food, right? And sometimes great food served simply is the way to go. I stand by that.

Wash the potatoes well and cut into 1.5 cm thick chips. Place in a saucepan, cover with cold salted water and bring to the boil. When the water comes to the boil, drain the potatoes and transfer to a rack on a tray to cool. Chill in the fridge overnight, uncovered.

Heat the oil for deep-frying in a deep-fryer to 140°C (or in a heavy-based saucepan until a cube of bread browns in 35 seconds). Add the potato chips and deep-fry for 3 minutes. Remove with a slotted spoon and drain on paper towel, then chill in the fridge for a couple of minutes.

Preheat the oven to 180°C (fan-forced). Wrap the garlic cloves in foil and roast for 10–15 minutes or until soft. Allow to cool, then remove the skin and crush the flesh. Stir through the olive oil and set aside.

Shortly before you are ready to serve, reheat the deep-frying oil to 180°C (or until a cube of bread browns in 15 seconds). Add the chips and cook for 4 minutes or until golden and crisp. Remove with a slotted spoon and drain on paper towel.

Season the chips with salt and toss with the garlic oil, crumbled feta and oregano. Serve immediately.

Gigantes Jaffles
(see page 142)

Serves 4

100 g large dried lima
    (butter) beans
2½ tablespoons extra
    virgin olive oil
1 small brown onion, diced
½ carrot, diced
2 cloves garlic, crushed
100 ml white wine

100 g tinned crushed tomatoes
1 bay leaf
5 sprigs thyme, leaves picked
unsalted butter, for spreading
8 slices white bread
100 g grated kefalograviera
    cheese
salt flakes and cracked pepper

Gigantes jaffles

Pictured page 141

Yes, you are going to need a jaffle maker for this dish. Jaffles were a treat for us when we were growing up so I've always loved them – crunchy on the outside and soft in the middle. Yum. A little tip: never wash your jaffle maker. Just wipe it clean with a cloth and a little olive oil.

Soak the beans in water overnight. Drain, then cook in fresh water (without any salt) until tender. Leave to cool completely in the liquid.

Heat the olive oil in a medium saucepan over medium heat and saute the onion, carrot and garlic until softened. Pour in the white wine and simmer until reduced by half. Drain the beans, then add to the pan with the crushed tomatoes, bay leaf and thyme and simmer for 20 minutes. Remove and allow to cool, then chill in the fridge until needed.

Butter the bread on both sides. Place 2 tablespoons of the bean mixture on four of the bread slices, sprinkle with the kefalograviera cheese and season with salt and pepper. Top with a second slice of bread and cook in a jaffle maker until golden brown.

Serves 4

2 medium eggplants (aubergines)
2½ tablespoons extra virgin
  olive oil, plus extra to garnish
110 g tahini
juice of 1 large lemon
salt flakes
⅔ cup (100 g) pine nuts, toasted
⅓ cup (50 g) raisins
dill sprigs and apple mint leaves
  (or regular mint leaves),
  to garnish

Dirty eggplant, tahini, lemon, pine nuts, raisins

Pictured
Page 145

I'm not sure why I call this dirty eggplant – I guess it's the way the eggplants are cooked. You can use your oven if you like, but don't be afraid to fire up your barbecue. If you have a charcoal barbecue, so much the better.

Preheat a barbecue grill plate to high heat. Pierce the eggplants all over with the tip of a knife, then place on the grill and cook until blackened all over. (Alternatively, preheat the oven to 200°C (fan-forced) and roast the eggplants for 30 minutes.) Place the charred eggplants in a bowl, cover with plastic film and rest for 15 minutes.

Remove the skin and discard any resting juices. Cut the eggplants in half, then press flat with your hand to spread them out.

Combine the olive oil, tahini, lemon juice and 3–4 tablespoons water in a small bowl and season with salt.

Dress the pine nuts and raisins with a little dressing, the drizzle the rest over the eggplant halves. Top with the fresh herbs, drizzle with a little extra olive oil and serve.

Dirty eggplant, tahini,
lemon, pine nuts, raisins
(see page 143)

Serves 4

4 small pita breads (see page 289)
extra virgin olive oil, for brushing
salt flakes and cracked pepper
100 g natural Greek-style yoghurt
juice of 1 lemon
coriander and mint leaves,
 to garnish
lemon wedges, to serve

Kofta

½ teaspoon coriander seeds
1 tablespoon extra virgin olive oil
200 g minced lamb
40 g crustless white bread,
 soaked in water and
 squeezed out
½ small brown onion, finely diced
2 cloves garlic, crushed
¼ teaspoon salt flakes
⅛ teaspoon cracked pepper

Open pita kofta, mint, lemon yoghurt

This is a very loose interpretation of kofta, so it's not traditional at all but wonderfully easy to make. My mum would have a stack of these in the fridge ready to go so when we came home we could cook them ourselves. It's funny, I never really cooked as a kid – Mum would always do it for us.

Preheat the oven to 180°C (fan-forced).

To make the kofta, crush the coriander seeds in a mortar and pestle. Heat the olive oil in a small frying pan and lightly cook the seeds until fragrant. Place in a bowl with the lamb, bread, onion, garlic, salt and pepper and mix well with your hands (use kitchen gloves for this). Divide the kofta mixture into four portions, then mould into discs a similar size to the bread.

Brush the pita breads with a little olive oil and brown on one side in a frying pan. Top the unbrowned side with the kofta discs (like a pizza). Transfer to a large baking tray and rest for 10 minutes. Brush with olive oil and season with salt and pepper, then bake for 10 minutes.

Whisk together the yoghurt and lemon juice and season to taste.

Drizzle the lemon yoghurt over the kofta pita breads and garnish with coriander and mint leaves. Serve immediately with lemon wedges.

Fried egg, sautéed greens,
tomato sauce (see page 150)

Serves 4

⅓ cup (80 ml) extra virgin olive oil
2 tablespoons sherry vinegar
salt flakes and cracked
    white pepper
4 eggs
black Cypriot salt, to garnish

Tomato sauce
½ cup (125 ml) extra virgin
    olive oil
1 brown onion, diced
1 clove garlic, thinly sliced

1 bay leaf
1 teaspoon dried oregano
2 medium tomatoes,
    roughly chopped
2 teaspoons raw sugar
salt flakes and cracked pepper

Sauteed greens
½ bunch silverbeet (Swiss chard)
1 bunch kale
1 bunch cavolo nero

Fried egg, Sauteed greens, Tomato Sauce

Pictured page 149

You may be thinking there's a lot of olive oil in this recipe but you really do need it all. Extra virgin olive oil is a must in Hellenic cooking. I remember my yia yia (maternal grandmother) telling me that when she came to Australia in the 1970s the only place you could get it from was the chemist as it was more commonly used for medicinal purposes. Times have certainly changed. Go nuts! Use lots of it – it's so good for you and tastes amazing.

To make the tomato sauce, heat the olive oil in a frying pan over medium heat and saute the onion, garlic, bay leaf and oregano until softened. Add the tomato and sugar and cook until the liquid has reduced by a third. Season to taste with salt and pepper.

For the sauteed greens, bring a large saucepan of salted water to the boil. Prepare the greens by removing the leaves from the stalks and washing them thoroughly. Set the stalks aside. Blanch the leaves in the boiling water for 3 minutes, then remove and refresh in iced water. Repeat the process with the stalks. Drain and dry well, then roughly chop the leaves and cut the stalks into 1–2 cm pieces.

Heat 2 tablespoons olive oil in a large frying pan until slightly smoking and saute the greens (leaves and stalks). Add the tomato sauce and stir to combine. Season with the sherry vinegar, salt and white pepper.

Heat the remaining olive oil in a smaller frying pan and fry the eggs until cooked to your liking.

Divide the tomato mixture among serving plates, top each with a fried egg and finish with a sprinkling of black Cypriot salt.

Serves 2

1 loukaniko (Greek sausage)
2 red bull horn chillies
2 medium kipfler potatoes
4 eggs
2–3 tablespoons roughly
   chopped flat-leaf parsley
1/8 teaspoon cracked pepper
salt flakes
2 tablespoons extra virgin olive oil

Greek Sausage, bull horn chilli, potato omelette

Pictured page 153

Loukaniko is a classic Cypriot sausage made with pork or beef mixed with cinnamon, cloves, fennel seed and coriander seed. If you can't get hold of them just use one of your favourite sausages. The bull horn chillies are lovely as they more about flavour than heat.

Preheat the oven to 180°C (fan-forced).

Cut the loukaniko in half lengthways and then into 5 mm thick slices. Cut the bull horn chillies to the same size.

Place the whole potatoes in a saucepan of cold salted water and bring to the boil, then reduce the heat and simmer for 15 minutes or until tender. Drain and allow to cool slightly, then peel and cut into pieces the same size as the loukaniko.

In a medium bowl, whisk the eggs and parsley and season with pepper and 1/4 teaspoon salt.

Heat the olive oil in a small (15 cm) ovenproof non-stick frying pan over medium heat. Saute the loukaniko, chilli and potato, then add the egg mixture and cook for 2 minutes. Transfer to the oven and cook for a further 3 minutes or until firm. Sprinkle with salt and serve hot.

Greek sausage,
bull horn chilli,
potato omelette (see page 151)

Serves 4

Pasticcio croquettes

2½ tablespoons extra
   virgin olive oil
250 g minced pork
125 g minced beef
½ brown onion, finely diced
2 cloves garlic, finely chopped
1 tablespoon tomato paste
   (puree)
100 ml white wine
200 ml chicken stock
   (see page 298)
1 cinnamon stick
½ teaspoon dried mint
1 teaspoon raw sugar

salt flakes
100 g macaroni
2 eggs
1 cup (150 g) plain flour
100 g panko breadcrumbs
vegetable oil, for deep-frying
grated kefalograviera and
   Japanese mayonnaise, to serve

Bechamel
50 g unsalted butter
⅓ cup (50 g) plain flour
325 ml full-cream milk

I hate waste. My mother always taught me that you should never waste food. We are lucky to have it so we should always respect it. Chefs who throw food out get a yellow card from me and if they get a second it's a red card, and you know what happens next. This recipe is also a great way to use up leftover pasticcio (see page 79), if you have some. My preference is to use the panko crumbs here rather than regular breadcrumbs as they give the croquettes a nice crunchy coating.

Heat the olive oil in a large saucepan over medium heat and saute the pork and beef mince until cooked through, breaking up any lumps with a wooden spoon. Add the onion and garlic and cook for 2 minutes, then stir in the tomato paste and cook for a further 2 minutes. Add the wine and cook until it has evaporated, then add the stock and cinnamon stick and simmer over low heat for 10 minutes or until all the moisture has evaporated. Stir in the dried mint, sugar and ¼ teaspoon salt and set aside.

To make the bechamel, place the butter in a small saucepan and melt over low heat. Add the flour and cook for 3 minutes, stirring constantly. Gradually add the milk, whisking constantly to avoid any lumps forming. Reduce the heat and simmer gently for 10–15 minutes or until thickened, stirring frequently.

Meanwhile, cook the macaroni in boiling salted water for 8–10 minutes or until al dente. Drain.

Place the meat mixture, bechamel and macaroni in a large bowl and mix well. Using a piping bag fitted with a large nozzle, pipe the mixture onto a lined baking tray in lengths about 1 cm thick. Place in the freezer until firm, then cut into 5–6 cm lengths (you'll need 12 croquettes all up).

Crack the eggs into a clean bowl and whisk with 1 tablespoon water to make an egg wash. Place the flour in a shallow bowl and the breadcrumbs in another bowl.

Roll the croquettes in the flour, then the egg wash and finally in the breadcrumbs.

Heat the oil for deep-frying in a deep-fryer to 180°C (or in a heavy-based saucepan until a cube of bread browns in 15 seconds). Add the croquettes in batches and cook for 3 minutes or until nicely golden. Remove with a slotted spoon and drain on paper towel.

Sprinkle the croquettes with kefalograviera and salt flakes and serve hot with Japanese mayonnaise.

Serves 4

vegetable oil, for deep-frying
200 g fresh whitebait
⅔ cup (100 g) cornflour
salt flakes
4 soft rolls, toasted
⅓ cup (100 g) mayonnaise
  (see page 292)
¼ head iceberg lettuce, shredded
1 red onion, sliced on a mandolin
large handful of coriander leaves
cracked pepper

Pickled carrot
1 carrot, grated
100 ml white wine vinegar
1 tablespoon brown sugar
1 star anise
6 juniper berries
2 white peppercorns
4–5 coriander stalks

Whitebait rolls, pickled carrot

Deep-fried whitebait is the quintessential Hellenic meze. It's what you nibble on while drinking a glass of ouzo. Here in Melbourne we can get it fresh and local, which is great, but I believe the lucky folks in New Zealand have the best whitebait in the world. Wherever you live, buy the best-quality fish you can find and reap the rewards with this moreish dish.

To make the pickled carrot, place the carrot in a heatproof bowl. Combine the vinegar, sugar, star anise, juniper berries, peppercorns, coriander stalks and 100 ml water in a medium saucepan. Bring to the boil, then remove from the heat and strain onto the grated carrot. Cover with plastic film and store in the fridge until needed.

Heat the oil for deep-frying in a deep-fryer to 180°C (or in a heavy-based saucepan until a cube of bread browns in 15 seconds).

Toss the whitebait in the cornflour, shaking off any excess, then add to the oil and deep-fry for 5 minutes or until crisp and golden. Remove with a slotted spoon and drain well on paper towel. Season with salt.

Cut the rolls in half. Spread 1 tablespoon mayo over the base of each roll, followed by the pickled carrot, whitebait, lettuce, red onion and coriander. Season with salt and pepper and serve hot.

Serves 4

4 corn cobs, husks on
1 tablespoon extra virgin olive oil
½ teaspoon smoked paprika
¼ teaspoon cayenne pepper
1 teaspoon salt flakes
⅓ cup (100 g) mayonnaise
  (see page 292)
1 cup (80 g) grated mizithra
  cheese
1 teaspoon fennel seeds, toasted

Chargrilled corn, mizithra, fennel seed, mayonnaise

This recipe is so nostalgic for me. It makes me think of winter on the steets of Athens, where little old men would barbecue corn on the cob and serve it sprinkled with salt. Delicious. If you can, barbecue the corn over wood – the flavour is much better that way. I guess you could say mizithra is the Greek version of parmesan so if you can't find it, parmesan will do (at a pinch!).

Bring a medium saucepan of water to the boil, add the corn cobs and blanch for 3 minutes. Peel the husk back from each cob, leaving it attached at the bottom. Lightly brush the corn with olive oil. Heat a chargrill pan or barbecue grill until hot and chargrill the corn for about 1 minute on each side or until slightly blackened and tender.

Meanwhile, combine the smoked paprika, cayenne pepper and salt.

Remove the corn from the heat, season with the spice mix and smear with mayonnaise. Top with grated cheese and finish with a sprinkling of fennel seeds.

Serves 4

500 g minced chicken
2 cloves garlic, finely chopped
2 tablespoons finely chopped
   coriander
2 tablespoons salted baby
   capers, rinsed and chopped
4 spring onions, thinly sliced
1 small brown onion, thinly sliced
2 tablespoons kecap manis
1 tablespoon peanut oil
300 g Chinese cabbage
   (wombok), finely shredded

1 tablespoon tapioca flour
1 egg white
salt flakes
12 wonton wrappers
1 egg yolk, lightly beaten

Dipping sauce
100 ml soy sauce
1½ tablespoons extra virgin
   olive oil

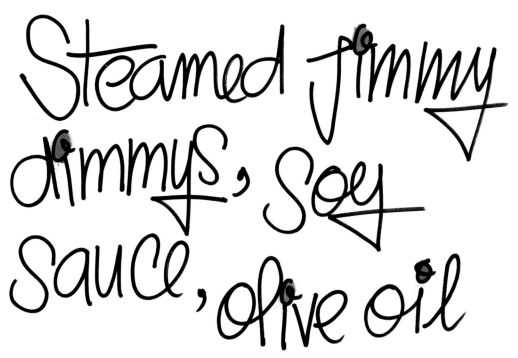

Steamed Jimmy Dimmys, Soy Sauce, olive oil

These are straight off the menu at Jimmy Grants, my souvlaki bar. You're probably wondering about the unlikely combination of Greek and Dimmys, but I say why not? The mixture of Greek olive oil and Chinese soy sauce absolutely makes the dish.

Place the chicken, garlic, coriander, capers, spring onion, onion, kecap manis, peanut oil, cabbage, tapioca flour, egg white and salt in a bowl and mix with your hands until well combined (use kitchen gloves for this).

Lay the wonton wrappers in a single layer on a clean surface. Place a tablespoon of the filling in the centre of each wrapper. Working with one wonton at a time, brush the edges with egg yolk and bring the edges up to tightly enclose the filling. Press to seal.

Line a steamer basket with baking paper. Arrange the wontons in a single layer in the basket, seam-side down, leaving a space between each one. (Depending on the size of your steamer, you may need to do this in batches.) Place the basket over a wok of simmering water (making sure the water doesn't touch the base), then cover and steam for 8–10 minutes or until cooked through. Transfer to a serving plate and cover loosely with foil to keep warm.

To make the dipping sauce, whisk together the soy sauce and olive oil.

Serve the wontons warm with the dipping sauce.

Serves 4

8 chicken thigh fillets
salt flakes

Marinade
1 brown onion, roughly chopped
2 large handfuls of flat-leaf
   parsley leaves
1 bunch oregano, leaves picked

2 cloves garlic, peeled and
   left whole
2 teaspoons dried oregano
1 teaspoon black peppercorns,
   crushed
2 teaspoons aleppo flakes
1 cup (250 ml) olive oil

Chicken spit

Quintessentially Greek, 'the spit' is not really about the food, it's about the ceremony of lighting the fire and getting it right. Then once the fire is right, it's about men standing around basting and protecting the spit from invaders. Not sure why exactly – it's just a Greek thing. It's important to give the chicken plenty of time to marinate, so start the recipe a day ahead. And make sure you season the chicken with salt once it is over the spit to keep it as moist as possible.

To make the marinade, put all the ingredients in a blender and blend to a smooth green paste. You don't need to add any salt to the marinade.

Rub the marinade into the chicken thighs, then cover and marinate in the fridge overnight.

When you're ready to cook, fold the thighs and thread evenly onto the spit. Place over the fire and season well with salt flakes. Cook for 60–70 minutes or until caramelised and cooked through. Serve hot.

Serves 4

250 g coarsely minced pork
250 g coarsely minced beef
1 large brown onion, grated
2 handfuls of flat-leaf parsley,
    roughly chopped
1 teaspoon roughly chopped mint
2 teaspoons salt flakes
2 teaspoons ground cinnamon

½ teaspoon cracked pepper
1 teaspoon baking powder
2 large eggs
4 potatoes, grated, excess liquid
    squeezed out
vegetable oil, for pan-frying
flat-leaf parsley and chervil,
    to garnish (optional)

Cypriot
keftedes

MC : **I used to make these often, especially when George was little. They're really nice served simply with a rice pilaf, chips and salad, or bottom of the salad oils and vinegar (see page 219), and George used to love the leftovers the next day wrapped in crusty bread. Take care that you don't fry the keftedes too hard – gentle is the way to go.**

Place all the ingredients (except the oil) in a bowl and mix together well. Leave to stand at room temperature for 30 minutes, then form tablespoons of the mixture into football shapes (you should have enough to make about 16 keftedes).

Pour the vegetable oil into a frying pan to a depth of 2–3 cm and place over medium heat. Add the keftedes and cook for 10–12 minutes or until golden and cooked through. Remove and drain on paper towel, then serve hot, garnished with parsley and chervil (if using).

1 bunch silverbeet (Swiss chard), well washed
500 g minced pork
500 g minced veal
2 tablespoons roughly chopped flat-leaf parsley
2 tablespoons tomato paste (puree)

1 tablespoon dried mint
1 cup (150 g) finely chopped vine-ripened tomatoes
½ cup (100 g) long-grain rice, washed well and drained
juice of 1 large lemon
salt flakes and cracked pepper
2 egg whites

Silverbeet Koupepia

MC: Koupepia are the Cypriot version of dolmades. They can be made with vine leaves, of course, but I like to wrap them in silverbeet. It is really important to leave the koupepia in the pan after cooking, so they absorb all the juices and flavours as they cool down. These are best served at room temperature.

Cook the silverbeet in batches in a large saucepan of boiling water for 2–3 minutes or until softened. Remove and refresh in cold water.

Heat a large frying pan over medium heat. Add the mince (you don't need any oil) and cook gently until browned, breaking up any lumps with a wooden spoon. Add the remaining ingredients (except the egg whites) and mix well. Remove from the heat and leave the mixture to cool completely, then stir in the egg whites.

When you are ready to start rolling, lay a piece of silverbeet on a chopping board and remove the white stalk with a sharp knife, leaving only the green leaf. Place a heaped tablespoon of the filling on one end of the silverbeet and roll up like a cigar, bringing in the sides to enclose about two-thirds of the way along. Repeat with the remaining silverbeet and filling.

Transfer the rolls to a heavy-based saucepan, seam-side down, placing a heatproof plate on top to keep them in place and help maintain their shape. Pour hot water over to completely cover. Put the lid on and bring to the boil, then reduce the heat and simmer for 30 minutes or until the rice is cooked. Turn off the heat and leave the rolls to cool in the liquid. Once cool, remove from the pan with tongs and serve.

Makes 14–16

1 tablespoon extra virgin olive oil
250 g minced beef
1 brown onion, very finely chopped
2–3 tablespoons finely chopped
    flat-leaf parsley
½ teaspoon ground cinnamon
¼ teaspoon freshly grated
    nutmeg
salt flakes and cracked pepper
2 tablespoons blanched almonds,
    roughly chopped (optional)
1 egg yolk, lightly beaten
vegetable oil, for pan-frying

Pastry
3 cups (450 g) plain flour
½ teaspoon salt flakes
½ cup (125 ml) vegetable oil

Mincemeat pastries

(MC): These pastries
(bourekia) are a great snack
to have on hand, or to take
to a friend's house as a gift.
I believe that food that you
have made with your own
hands, with love and care, is
one of the best gifts you can
give another person. All these
boureki need is a nice bowl
of yoghurt on the side to dip
them into.

To make the pastry, sift the flour into a bowl and add the salt, then rub in
the oil with your fingertips. Gradually add 150 ml cold water to bring the
pastry together (you may not need it all). The dough should be quite soft.
Knead for 5 minutes, then cover with a clean tea towel and rest at room
temperature for 30 minutes.

Heat the olive oil in a large frying pan over medium heat, add the mince
and cook gently until browned, breaking up any lumps with a wooden
spoon. Add the onion and parsley and cook until the onion has softened.
Stir in the cinnamon and nutmeg and season well with salt and pepper,
then set aside to cool. Mix in the almonds (if using).

Roll out the pastry using a pasta machine or with a rolling pin, until very
thin (about 1 mm if you can). Place teaspoons of the filling along one half
of the pastry, working in a line and leaving a 3 cm gap between each one,
then brush around the filling with egg yolk.

Fold the sheet of pastry over to cover the filling, then cut with a sharp
knife to the desired size and press on the ends firmly with a fork to seal.

Pour the vegetable oil into a frying pan to a depth of 2 cm, add the
pastries and cook over medium–high heat for 1–2 minutes each side or
until golden and cooked through. Remove with a slotted spoon and drain
on paper towel. Serve hot or cold.

Serves 4

4 good-sized globe artichokes
1 tablespoon lemon juice
1 tablespoon extra virgin olive oil,
   plus extra to serve
1 tablespoon salt flakes
2 tablespoons finely chopped
   flat-leaf parsley
black Cypriot salt, to garnish

Artichoke soaking water
2 tablespoons plain flour
juice of 1 lemon
2 tablespoon salt flakes

Egg and lemon sauce
2 cups (500 ml) chicken stock
   (see page 298)
1 tablespoon cornflour
3 egg yolks
2 tablespoons lemon juice
salt flakes and cracked
   white pepper

Artichokes with egg and lemon Sauce

MC : George doesn't like that I use flour to prepare my artichokes but hey, it's my recipe not his. I was taught that adding flour to the soaking liquid helps to keep them white, so that is what I do.

This dish is all about celebrating artichokes when they are in season, as they are not here for long. The avgolemono is a simple sauce of eggs, stock and lemon juice, and it must be light and fluffy. Be careful not to heat the sauce too much otherwise it will curdle.

To prepare the artichoke soaking water, blend the flour with a little water, then add to a bowl of chilled water with the lemon juice and salt.

Using a sharp paring knife, trim off the leaves and the inner flower from each artichoke, until just the heart remains. Leave 4 cm of the stalk and peel it with a vegetable peeler. Place each artichoke in the soaking water as you finish it so they don't start to turn brown.

Bring a large saucepan of water to the boil and add the lemon juice, olive oil and salt flakes. Add the prepared artichokes and cook for 5 minutes or until tender. Remove and drain well on paper towel, then place on a serving dish.

To make the sauce, bring the chicken stock to the boil in a clean saucepan. Blend the cornflour with a little water to form a paste, then gradually add this to the stock, whisking constantly until smooth and slightly thickened. Boil for 2 minutes, then remove from the heat. In a bowl, whisk together the egg yolks and lemon juice, then whisk this into the stock. Return the pan to the heat for 1 minute, without boiling, and season to taste with salt and pepper.

Pour the sauce over the artichokes and sprinkle with parsley. Finish with a drizzle of olive oil and some black Cypriot salt and serve.

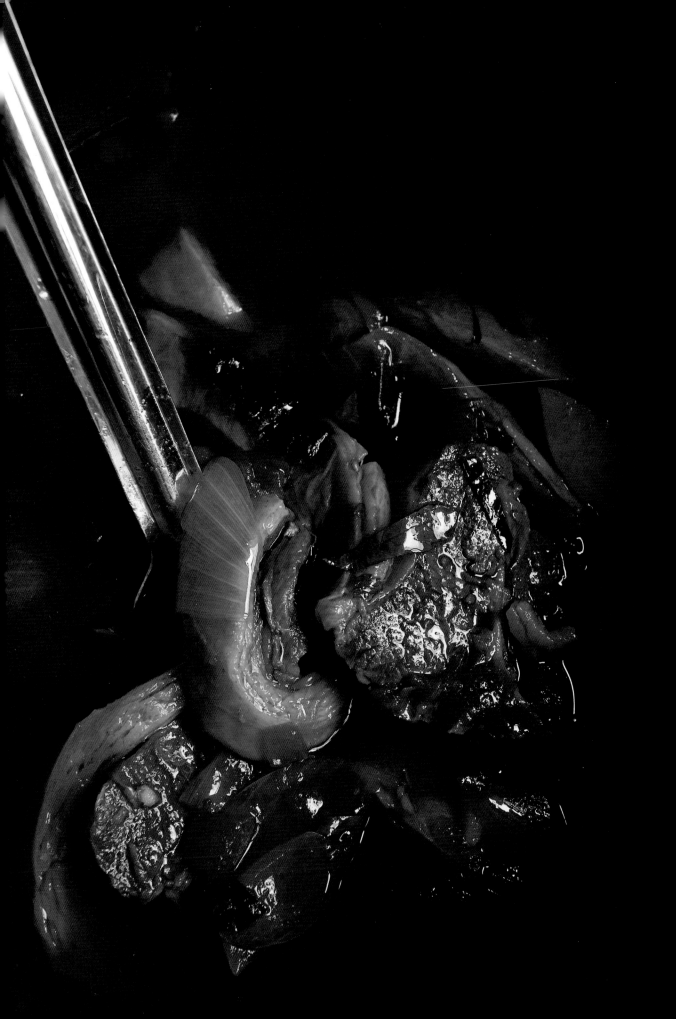

Cypriot tavas
(see page 184)

Serves 4

1 tablespoon cumin seeds
8 large lamb loin chops
3 large brown onions,
 thickly sliced
5 potatoes, cut into large chunks
6 large tomatoes, peeled
 and grated
2 teaspoons salt flakes

1 teaspoon cracked pepper
2 tablespoons tomato paste
 (puree), diluted in 1 cup
 (250 ml) hot water
¼ cup (60 ml) extra virgin
 olive oil
chopped flat-leaf parsley,
 to garnish

Pictured
page 183

Cypriot tavas

MC : Tavas is a classic Cypriot dish of slow-cooked lamb and vegetables, so inevitably I was taught how to cook it when I was a little girl. The food of my mother country is simple and generally made with inexpensive ingredients – homely food, but with lots of love in it.

All ovens are different so it is important that you cook with all your senses. Check the meat and vegetables regularly until they are cooked and tender, and add a little more water if needed so they don't dry out. This dish is delicious served simply with crusty bread and salad.

Preheat the oven to 180°C (fan-forced).

Toast the cumin seeds in a hot frying pan until lightly toasted and fragrant, then lightly crush in a mortar and pestle.

Place all the ingredients (except the olive oil and parsley) and 1.75 litres water in a large ovenproof dish and mix together well. Pour the olive oil over the top, then cover with foil and bake for 30 minutes.

Reduce the oven temperature to 160°C (fan-forced) and bake for a further 1 hour. Remove the foil and check the meat and vegetables are cooked through, then uncover and cook for another 15 minutes. Serve hot, garnished with parsley.

Serves 8

1.5 kg kolokassi (Cypriot taro)
1½ tablespoons extra virgin
   olive oil
1 kg boned pork shoulder,
   cut into 3 cm dice
1 small brown onion, finely diced
2–3 sticks celery, cut into
   3 cm chunks

¼ cup (70 g) tomato paste
   (puree), diluted in 1 cup
   (250 ml) hot water
salt flakes and cracked pepper
½ cup (125 ml) lemon juice
radishes and crusty bread,
   to serve

kolokassi with pork

Pictured page 187

MC: **George hates this dish and never ate it growing up, but for me it has Cyprus stamped all over it. Taro root is often used in our traditional recipes, but you must use the Cypriot variety and not the Asian as it will fall apart. What makes this dish so delicious is that the taro takes on all the flavour from the pork, giving a rich and satisfying result. Please don't listen to George – I promise you will love this.**

Scrub the kolokassi and dry well with paper towel. Do not wash it as it will become slimy if water touches it. With a thick-bladed knife cut down and turn 90 degrees so that the kolokassi breaks into a piece. Continue cutting around the kolokassi clockwise, trying to keep the pieces the same size as the pork.

Heat the olive oil in a heavy-based saucepan and cook the pork until browned all over. Remove to a plate, then add the onion and cook until softened. Add the celery and cook for a few minutes, stirring occasionally. Return the pork to the pan.

Add the tomato paste mixture and enough water to cover, and season well with salt and pepper. Bring to the boil, then reduce the heat and simmer for 30 minutes. Add the kolokassi and top up with enough water to cover, then simmer for a further 1 hour, checking the water level from time to time.

Check that the pork and kolokassi are nice and tender, then add the lemon juice and adjust the seasoning if needed. Serve with fresh radishes and crusty bread.

Kolokassi with pork
(see page 185)

A DISH FOR JAMES AND MICHAELA

Words cannot explain what these two little creatures mean to me. They are my everything and I would die for them. Natalie and I are the luckiest people on earth to have them, and I am just as lucky to have Natalie, who is the best mother to those kids. She is the glue that keeps everything together, through her support and guidance.

I'm often asked which school they will go to. I am not fussed about fancy schools – I am more driven to teach my kids the art of hospitality. The lessons I have learnt in restaurants are priceless and have made me the person I am today. I have learnt to be street wise and understand that you have to work hard if you want something. Nothing is easy in life. Nothing. But if you love it and dream it, it will happen.

This dish is not Greek but it has the loving Greek heart that I was always taught when I was a little boy.

Cruskits with avocado, tomato and parmesan

Serves 2

1 avocado
a pinch of salt flakes
juice of ½ lemon
1 ripe tomato
1 teaspoon Vegemite, or to taste
4 Cruskits
grated parmesan, to serve

Peel the avocado and remove the stone, then smash it with the back of a fork until chunky and soft. Stir through the salt and lemon juice.

Cut the tomato in half and squeeze the pulp and seeds into a bowl.

To assemble, spread Vegemite over each Cruskit and top with about 1 tablespoon of the avocado mixture. Spoon 1 teaspoon of the tomato pulp over each Cruskit and finish with a liberal grating of parmesan.

Serves 4–6

20 baby qukes (baby cucumbers)
1 bunch dill, sprigs removed
    and reserved
2 cups (500 ml) champagne
    vinegar
1 tablespoon honey
20 coriander seeds
3 star anise
10 cardamom pods
¼ cup (30 g) salt flakes
10 white peppercorns
½ cup (125 ml) ouzo
extra virgin olive oil, for drizzling

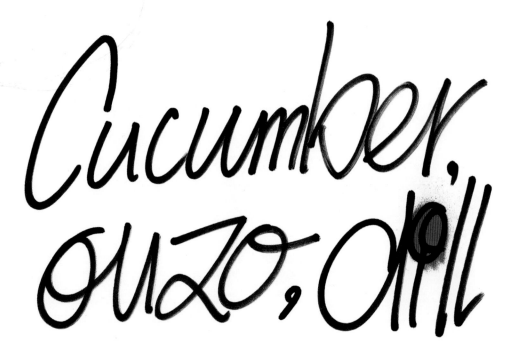

Cucumber, ouzo, dill

Ouzo and cucumbers for me is like basil and tomatoes for the Italians. The combination is so yum and just thinking about it makes me hungry. Make sure you pinprick the qukes so they take on the flavour of the cooking liquid. Serve the cucumbers straight from the fridge so they're nice and cold.

Pinprick the qukes about a dozen times all over.

Place the dill stalks in a large saucepan with the vinegar, honey, spices, salt, peppercorns, ouzo and 2 cups (500 ml) water. Bring to the boil.

Place the qukes in a heatproof bowl. Pour the boiling liquid through a fine sieve over the qukes, then cover the bowl tightly with plastic film and leave to cool. When cool, transfer to the fridge until needed (they will keep for up to 2 weeks).

To serve, remove the qukes from the liquid and place in a shallow bowl. Cut them up if you like, or leave them whole. Drizzle with a little olive oil and garnish with the reserved dill sprigs.

Serves 4

2 bunches heirloom dutch carrots
2 bunches heirloom purple carrots
1 clove garlic
¼ cup (60 ml) extra virgin olive oil
salt flakes and cracked pepper
½ cup (50 g) toasted salted walnuts
dill sprigs, to garnish

Whipped feta
200 g feta (I like Dodoni brand)
2 tablespoons full-cream milk

Dressing
1 tablespoon honey
1 tablespoon lemon juice
salt flakes and cracked pepper

Roasted heirloom carrots, whipped feta, toasted walnuts

These days salads can be so much more than green leaves in a bowl with vinaigrette. They should be all about great ingredients and have lots of texture. Is this recipe based on a classic Greek salad? NO. Does it taste amazing? Absolutely! Make sure the carrots are cooked all the way through so they're nice and tender, and serve them at room temperature. It's by far the best way to enjoy them.

Preheat the oven to 170°C (fan-forced).

Trim the carrots, so that only 1 cm of the stalk remains. Wash the carrots very well, especially around the stalks.

In a mortar and pestle, crush the garlic with the olive oil and a good pinch of salt and pepper too.

Toss the carrots in a bowl with the garlic oil, then spread out on a baking tray and roast for 15–30 minutes or until just tender. Allow to cool to room temperature.

Meanwhile, to make the whipped feta, place the feta and milk in a blender and blend until completely smooth. Chill until needed.

Remove the carrots from the baking tray, reserving the oil and pan juices, and transfer to a plate.

To make the dressing, whisk together the honey, lemon juice and reserved oil and pan juices, and season to taste.

Spoon the whipped feta onto the plate, top with the carrots and drizzle with the dressing. Scatter over the walnuts and dill sprigs, and serve.

Roast beetroot, pearl barley, peanut hummus
(see page 198)

Serves 4

4 medium beetroots, trimmed
  and washed
¼ cup (50 g) pearl barley
100 g peanut and coriander-seed
  hummus (see page 51)
50 g unsalted peanuts
juice of ½ lemon

salt flakes and cracked pepper
2½ tablespoons extra virgin
  olive oil
1 teaspoon dried mountain
  oregano
watercress and oregano leaves,
  to garnish

Pictured
Page 197

Roast beetroot, pearl barley, peanut hummus

The recipe asks for mountain oregano which literally means what it says: oregano that grows in the mountains of Greece. If you can't get your hands on any, just use regular dried oregano. I am not really into dried herbs as a rule, but I do love dried mint and oregano.

Preheat the oven to 180°C (fan-forced).

Place the beetroot on a baking tray and roast for 25–35 minutes or until soft enough for a skewer to pass through easily. While hot, peel the beetroots and cut into large pieces.

Pour the pearl barley into a small sauepan and add ½ cup (125 ml) cold water. Bring to the boil, then reduce the heat and simmer for 15 minutes or until tender, topping up the water if needed. Drain and set aside.

Using a stick blender, blend the hummus, peanuts and a squeeze of lemon juice until smooth. Season with salt.

Whisk together the olive oil, dried oregano and remaining lemon juice to make a dressing, and season with salt and pepper.

Toss the dressing through the beetroot and pearl barley. Spoon the peanut hummus onto a serving plate and top with the beetroot salad. Garnish with watercress and oregano leaves and serve.

Serves 4

100 g blackcurrants
½ baby blue pumpkin
2½ tablespoons extra virgin
   olive oil
salt flakes and cracked pepper
4–5 tablespoons mixed seeds,
   including sesame, sunflower
   and pumpkin seeds

8 spring onions, thinly sliced
   on an angle
1 tablespoon chardonnay vinegar
100 g goat's curd

Charred pumpkin, goat's curd

Pictured page 200

Pumpkin and goat's curd is a great combination, both for flavour and texture. Make sure the pumpkin is soft and cooked through – nothing worse than raw pumpkin.

Preheat the oven to 160°C (fan-forced) and line a baking tray with baking paper.

Soak the blackcurrants in warm water until plumped up.

Cut the pumpkin into 5–6 cm thick wedges, removing the seeds but keeping the skin on. Rub with half the olive oil.

Heat a chargrill pan or barbecue grill until hot. Grill the pumpkin to obtain nice char marks on both sides. Transfer the pumpkin to the prepared baking tray and season with salt and pepper. Bake for 12–15 minutes or until the flesh is soft when tested with a knife.

Toast the seed mix in a dry frying pan over medium heat for 2–3 minutes or until lightly golden. Keep the pan moving so they don't stick to the bottom and burn. Remove and cool in a bowl.

Drain the blackcurrants and combine in a bowl with the spring onion. Dress with the chardonnay vinegar and remaining olive oil, and season to taste.

Place the pumpkin on a plate and top with the spring onion salad. Pipe or spoon the goat's curd around the plate and serve.

Salates – 199

charred pumpkin, goat's curd

(see page 199)

Serves 4

2 tablespoons extra virgin olive oil
1 brown onion, diced
300 ml pure cream (45% fat)
500 g cauliflower, trimmed and
    cut into small florets
1½ cups (240 g) green peas
50 g blanched almonds
vegetable oil, for deep-frying
large handful of pea
    tendrils (optional)

Oregano salt
¼ teaspoon dried oregano
¼ teaspoon salt flakes
¼ teaspoon caster sugar

Lemon dressing
1 tablespoon lemon juice
2½ tablespoons extra
    virgin olive oil

Garden peas, cauliflower, almonds, Lemon

You may have heard of the saying 'when it rains pumpkins, make soup and sell it'. Well in the same spirit I say when peas are in season, make this salad. It's colourful, super-fresh and really yummy. For maximum flavour, make sure the peas are at room temperature when you serve the salad.

Heat the olive oil in a frying pan over medium heat, add the onion and cook until translucent. Add the cream and half the cauliflower and simmer gently over low heat for 10–12 minutes or until tender, stirring frequently to avoid any colouration. Strain, reserving the cooking liquid. Transfer the cauliflower and onion to a blender and blend to a smooth puree, adding a little of the reserved cooking liquid as required.

Bring a small saucepan of water to the boil and cook the peas for 1 minute, then refresh in iced water. Drain.

Preheat the oven to 160°C (fan-forced).

To make the oregano salt, combine the dried oregano, salt and sugar in a small bowl.

Toast the almonds in the oven for 10 minutes or until golden, then roughly chop and season with a little oregano salt.

To make the lemon dressing, whisk together the lemon juice and olive oil. Season to taste with oregano salt.

Heat the oil for deep-frying in a deep-fryer to 180°C (or in a heavy-based saucepan until a cube of bread browns in 15 seconds). Add the remaining cauliflower florets and deep-fry until golden. Remove with a slotted spoon and drain on paper towel. Season with oregano salt.

In a mixing bowl, combine the peas, cauliflower florets, almonds and lemon dressing.

Spoon the cauliflower puree onto a serving place, top with the mixed salad and garnish with young pea tendrils (if using). Serve cold.

Smoked octopus, kipflers, crispy chicken skin
(see page 206)

Serves 6

600 g large octopus tentacles,
   tenderised
finely grated zest and juice
   of 1 lemon
1 tablespoon fennel seeds
100 ml extra virgin olive oil
handful of wood chips
400 g kipfler potatoes

8 spring onions, sliced on
   an angle
80 g mayonnaise (see page 292)
salt flakes and cracked pepper
100 g crispy chicken skin
   (see page 58)

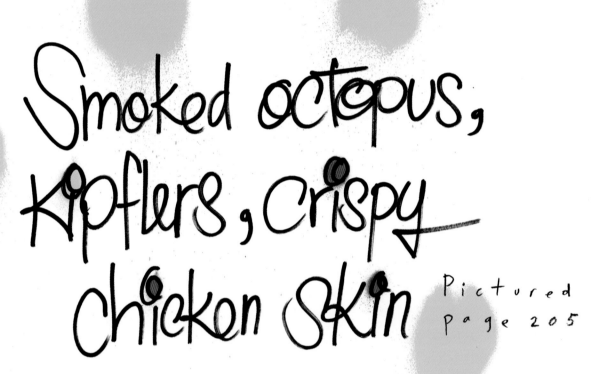

Smoked octopus, Kipflers, crispy chicken skin

Pictured page 205

Once you learn a new cooking technique you have it for life, and smoking food is a great one to have in your culinary backpack. It may seem daunting at first, but don't let it scare you off. The simple rule is when it smells nice it will taste nice. Make sure you get your fishmonger to beat your octopus for you. This will tenderise the meat, ensuring a great result for the chef.

Preheat the oven to 130°C (fan-forced).

Combine the octopus, lemon zest and juice, fennel seeds and olive oil in a shallow baking dish, cover with foil and bake for 1½ hours. Remove the octopus from the braise, discarding the liquid, and chill in the fridge.

Heat a barbecue until hot and place a layer of foil over the grill. Place the wood chips on the foil and light them, then close the lid of the barbecue. The flames should burn out. Open the lid and place the octopus in the barbecue on a wire rack, then close the lid and leave to smoke for 2 minutes. Remove the octopus and chill in the fridge until needed.

Place the potatoes in a saucepan of cold salted water. Bring to the boil, then reduce the heat and simmer for 10–15 minutes or until tender. Drain and set aside to cool, then remove the skin and cut into small pieces.

Slice the smoked octopus into pieces similar in size to the potato. Combine in a bowl with the potato, spring onion and mayonnaise. Season to taste and garnish with crispy chicken skin.

Serves 8

¼ cup (60 ml) balsamic vinegar
2 tablespoons honey
1 tablespoon Dijon mustard
¾ cup (185 ml) extra virgin
  olive oil
salt flakes and cracked pepper
¼ purple cabbage, very finely
  shredded

¼ drumhead cabbage, very finely
  shredded
2–3 golden shallots, thinly sliced
2 tablespoons dill sprigs
2 tablespoons roughly chopped
  flat-leaf parsley
100 g kefalograviera cheese

Cabbage salad, balsamic, grated Kefalograviera

This simple salad is on the menu at Jimmy Grants. It doesn't take a genius to make it, but be sure to dress the salad just before you serve. It needs to be crunchy and fresh.

Whisk together the balsamic vinegar and honey until the honey has dissolved, then whisk in the mustard and slowly drizzle in the olive oil. Season to taste with salt and pepper.

Toss together the shredded cabbage, shallot, herbs and dressing. Season and transfer to a serving dish. Finely grate the kefalograviera over the top and serve.

Serves 4

1 iceberg lettuce
100 g kefalograviera cheese
lemon dressing (see page 202)
oregano leaves, to garnish
salt flakes or black Cypriot salt

Marouli Salad

Marouli means lettuce in Greek, so you get a sense of what the key ingredient will be! I like to keep the lettuce together rather that chopping it all up, but you can do it either way. The kefalograviera gives a lovely richness to the crisp leaves, making this salad pretty hard to resist. Dress it at the last minute to preserve the freshness.

Remove all the outer leaves from the lettuce and discard. Remove the core, then wash the lettuce in iced water. Drain or spin dry.

Cut the inner part of the lettuce into two 3–4 cm thick slices. Discard the remaining sides. Put the slices on a plate and grate the kefalograviera over the top. Drizzle with the lemon dressing and garnish with oregano leaves. Season with salt and serve.

Serves 4

¼ small watermelon
vegetable oil, for deep-frying
50 g vine leaves in brine
⅓ cup (50 g) plain flour
2 tablespoons extra virgin olive
   oil, plus extra to garnish
500 g calamari, cleaned, scored
   and cut into bite-sized pieces,
   tentacles reserved

salt flakes and cracked pepper
200 g green olives
200 g goat's curd, broken into
   small pieces
flat-leaf parsley, to garnish

Grilled calamari, watermelon, olives, goat's curd, crispy vine leaves

Throughout my career I've heard so many old wives' tales about cooking. I've been told to add oil to pasta water so the pasta won't stick. I've been told to add kiwi pulp to calamari to make it tender. All nonsense. All you need to remember is to buy fresh and in season and your calamari will be super-tender. The crispy vine leaves are not essential, but they are a great way to introduce saltiness to the dish.

Trim the skin from the watermelon and cut the flesh into thick rectangles about 15 cm × 5 cm. Store in the fridge until needed.

Heat the oil for deep-frying in a deep-fryer to 180°C (or in a heavy-based saucepan until a cube of bread browns in 15 seconds). Remove the vine leaves from the brine and pat dry with paper towel. Dust with flour, shaking off any excess, then deep-fry until crispy. Remove with a slotted spoon and drain on paper towel.

Meanwhile, heat a chargrill pan or barbecue grill or flatplate until hot. Drizzle the olive oil over the calamari and season with salt and pepper. Grill the calamari until lightly charred and the flesh has no transparency.

Arrange the watermelon, olives and goat's curd on a serving plate. Put the calamari and crisp vine leaves on top and finish with parsley leaves, a drizzle of olive oil and a final grinding of salt and pepper.

Serves 4

2 medium bulbs fennel, trimmed
2 blood oranges
1 tablespoon Santorini vinegar
2–3 tablespoons raisins
2½ tablespoons extra virgin
   olive oil
salt flakes and cracked pepper
2–3 tablespoons chervil,
   leaves picked

Shaved fennel, blood orange, Santorini vinegar raisins

Fennel is my favourite vegetable in the world. You can pretty much apply any cooking technique you like and it will be fabulous. This recipe is so simple to make, but the flavours are amazing. If you can't get hold of Santorini vinegar use a good cherry or even a raspberry vinegar instead.

Using a mandolin, finely shave the fennel straight into iced water.

Peel and segment the blood oranges, reserving the juices.

Mix 1 tablespoon of the reserved blood orange juice with the vinegar, raisins, olive oil, salt and pepper to make a dressing. Add the blood orange segments and chervil and toss gently to combine.

Drain the fennel and pat dry with paper towel.

Place the fennel in a serving bowl and top with orange salad, spooning any remaining dressing over the fennel.

LOVING MY PAST AND LEAVING MY EGO AT THE DOOR

My Dad always used to wait for us to finish the salad, then he would bring the bowl under his chin and dip his bread in the mixture of olive oil, vinegar and leftover bits of salad. This never made sense to me until I became older and wiser. It doesn't sound glamorous but can I tell you it tastes unreal. A young egotistical chef would certainly frown at this, as at that point in a chef's career all that matters is refinement and technique, and the need to show off. The ego of a chef is their worst enemy. You soon learn that humility, care and love unlock the secret to success. Lots and lots of love.

My food has changed over the years, and it's memories like this that have helped me understand how important my culture and past are for my future. Never disrespect the past and always to look to it for positive influences. Food is not about feeding your stomach, it's about taking you to an emotional place.

Bottom of the salad oils and vinegars, village bread

Serves 4 as a snack

½ red capsicum (pepper)
1 ripe tomato, seeds removed
½ bulb baby fennel, base trimmed
1 golden shallot
2 teaspoons salt flakes, or to taste
75 ml chardonnay vinegar
   (or any good-quality white
   wine vinegar)
1 cup (250 ml) extra virgin olive oil
village bread (see page 288),
   to serve

Place the capsicum under a hot grill until softened and collapsed. Remove and place in a bowl, then cover with plastic film and leave to sweat (this makes the skin easier to peel). When cooled, peel off the skin and remove and discard the seeds.

Place the capsicum, tomato, fennel, shallot, salt and vinegar in a blender and pulse until combined but not completely smooth. Transfer to a bowl and stir in the olive oil. The mixture should separate. Serve with village bread.

Bottom of the salad oils and vinegars,
village bread (see page 219)

Risogalo, salted caramel,
kourambiethes (See page 226)

Serves 4

120 g sushi rice
600 ml full-cream milk
pinch of salt flakes
1 vanilla bean, split,
    seeds scraped
50 g caster sugar
200 ml thickened cream,
    whipped to soft peaks
roughly chopped pistachios,
    to garnish

Salted caramel
400 g caster sugar
280 ml thickened cream

20 g unsalted butter, diced
1½ tablespoons salt flakes

Kourambiethes
170 g unsalted butter, softened
50 g caster sugar
1 vanilla bean, split,
    seeds scraped
125 g slivered almonds, toasted
125 g self-raising flour
⅔ cup (100 g) plain flour

Risogalo, Salted Caramel, Kourambiethes

Pictured page 225

I think just about every country in the world has a sweet rice dish. I guess it would stem from the tough times, but for me the Greek rice pudding, risogalo, represents honesty, warmth and generosity – three of the most important ingredients in cooking. If you don't cook with these, you are simply preparing food to fill your stomach.

Kourambiethes are Greek shortbreads often generously dusted with icing sugar. I include them here as a textural contrast to the creamy rice.

Place the rice and 480 ml cold water in a heavy-based saucepan and bring to the boil. Reduce the heat and simmer for 6 minutes, then drain, discarding the water. Return the rice to the saucepan, along with the milk, salt, vanilla bean and seeds. Bring back to the boil, then reduce to a gentle simmer and cook for 20 minutes or until the liquid has thickened and the rice is cooked. Add the sugar and stir until dissolved.

Pour the mixture into a flat dish or tray to cool, then cover with plastic film and chill in the fridge for 1 hour.

Meanwhile, to make the salted caramel, place the sugar and ½ cup (125 ml) water in a heavy-based saucepan over medium–high heat and stir until the sugar has dissolved, frequently brushing down the edges of the pan with a pastry brush dipped in water to prevent the sugar from crystallising. Once it has dissolved do not stir again. Gently boil until the caramel is golden brown (170°C on a sugar thermometer). Carefully pour in the cream and stir until combined. Remove the pan from the heat and whisk in the butter and salt. Pour onto a tray lined with baking paper and cool to room temperature.

For the kourambiethes, preheat the oven to 165°C (fan forced) and line a baking tray with baking paper. Place the butter, sugar, vanilla seeds and almonds in a large bowl and mix with your hands until the sugar has dissolved. Sift in the flours and continue to mix by hand until the mixture comes together. Spread out the dough on the prepared tray to a thickness of about 1 cm and bake for 12–15 minutes or until golden brown. Allow to cool, then gently break into large crumbs.

Transfer the chilled rice mixture to a bowl and stir to loosen. Remove the vanilla bean, then fold in the whipped cream.

To assemble, divide the rice pudding among four serving glasses, spoon over the salted caramel and scatter with kourambiethes and pistachios.

Serves 8

250 g skinned hazelnuts

Loukoumades
40 g dried yeast
2 teaspoons salt flakes
4⅓ cups (650 g) plain flour
vegetable oil, for deep-frying

Nutella and honey sauce
100 g Nutella or other chocolate
  and hazelnut spread
100 g honey

Loukoumades, honey, Nutella, toasted hazelnuts

Pictured page 228

This is very simple: take yummy Greek doughnuts (loukoumades) and toss them in a mixture of Nuttela and honey. Enough said. You need to really get into this recipe and use your hands, and make sure you make them on a Sunday afternoon. That's when my yia yia used to make them for me. Geez, I miss her.

To make the dough for the loukoumades, place the yeast, salt and 850 ml water in the bowl of an electric mixer and whisk by hand until the yeast has dissolved. Add the flour, then return the bowl to the mixer and mix using the whisk attachment for 10–15 minutes or until the dough is no longer sticking to the side of the bowl and forms into a ball. Transfer the dough to a larger bowl, cover with plastic film and set aside to prove for 2 hours or until doubled in size.

Meanwhile, preheat the oven to 180°C (fan-forced). Spread out the hazelnuts on a baking tray and toast for 5–10 minutes or until golden. Transfer to a food processor and blitz into chunky crumbs.

To make the sauce, place the Nutella, honey and 2 teaspoons water in a heatproof bowl set over a saucepan of barely simmering water (don't let the bottom of the bowl touch the water). Stir until melted and smooth.

Shortly before you are ready to serve, heat the oil for deep-frying in a deep-fryer to 180°C (or in a heavy-based saucepan until a cube of bread browns in 15 seconds). Meanwhile, firmly knead the dough to force any air out. Place the dough in a piping bag with a plain nozzle and, working in batches, pipe golf-ball-sized balls into the oil. Deep-fry until they are light golden and cooked through, then remove with a slotted spoon and drain on paper towel.

Arrange the loukoumades on a large platter, drizzle over the sauce and sprinkle with the hazelnut crumbs. Serve hot.

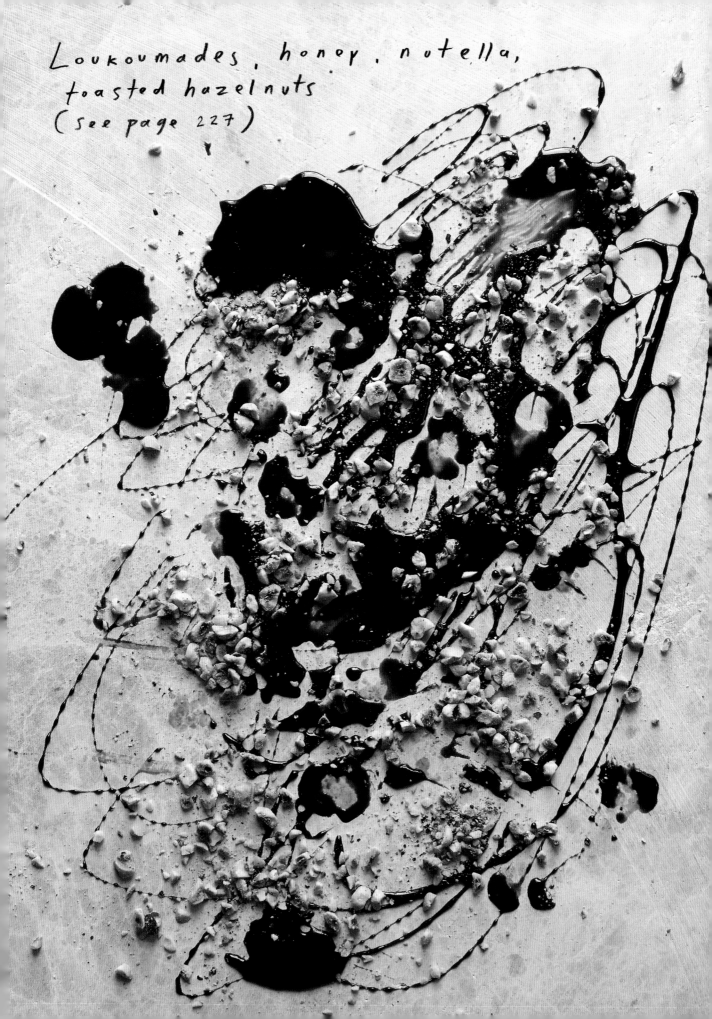

Loukoumades, honey, nutella,
toasted hazelnuts
(see page 227)

Serves 10

100 g caster sugar
2 small egg whites
  (you'll need 50 g in total)
1 teaspoon crushed freeze-dried
  raspberries
2 teaspoons crushed mastic
  musk stick (see page 237)
2½ tablespoons metaxa

Chocolate ice-cream
150 ml pure cream (45%)
350 ml full-cream milk
150 g egg yolks (from 7–8 eggs)
150 g caster sugar
400 g dark chocolate (70% cocoa
  solids), broken into pieces

Bombe metaxa

This is my play on the famous bombe Alaska. Metaxa is a fine Greek brandy that adds a unique flavour to the dish, but if alcohol is not your thing it's okay to leave it out. This is a great dessert to share and it will really test your cooking skills as it's all about getting the temperatures right when you assemble it.

To make the chocolate ice-cream, place the cream and milk in a heavy-based saucepan and gently bring to a simmer.

Meanwhile, whisk the egg yolks and sugar in a large heaproof bowl until the mixture becomes pale yellow. Slowly pour the cream mixture over the eggs, whisking constantly, then return the mixture to the pan and stir with a spatula over low heat until it is thick enough to coat the back of a spoon.

Place the chocolate in a heatproof bowl. Strain the custard through a fine-mesh sieve over the chocolate and stir until melted and smooth. Strain again, then chill in the fridge. When completely cold, transfer to an ice-cream machine and churn according to the manufacturer's instructions. Line 10 rice bowls with plastic film. When the ice-cream is stiff, spoon it into the prepared bowls and smooth the tops, then place in the freezer for 2 hours or until set.

When the ice-cream has set place the sugar and egg whites in a heatproof bowl set over a bowl of barely simmering water (don't let the bottom of the bowl touch the water). Whisk until the sugar has dissolved. Transfer to an electric mixer fitted with the whisk attachment and whisk until stiff peaks form. Gently fold in the raspberries and musk stick, then transfer the meringue to a piping bag with a 1 cm nozzle.

When you're ready to serve, turn out the chocolate ice-cream onto plates and pipe the meringue over the top. Pour the metaxa into a large steel kitchen spoon (1 teaspoon per bombe). Flambe with a match, then pour over the bombes in front of your guests.

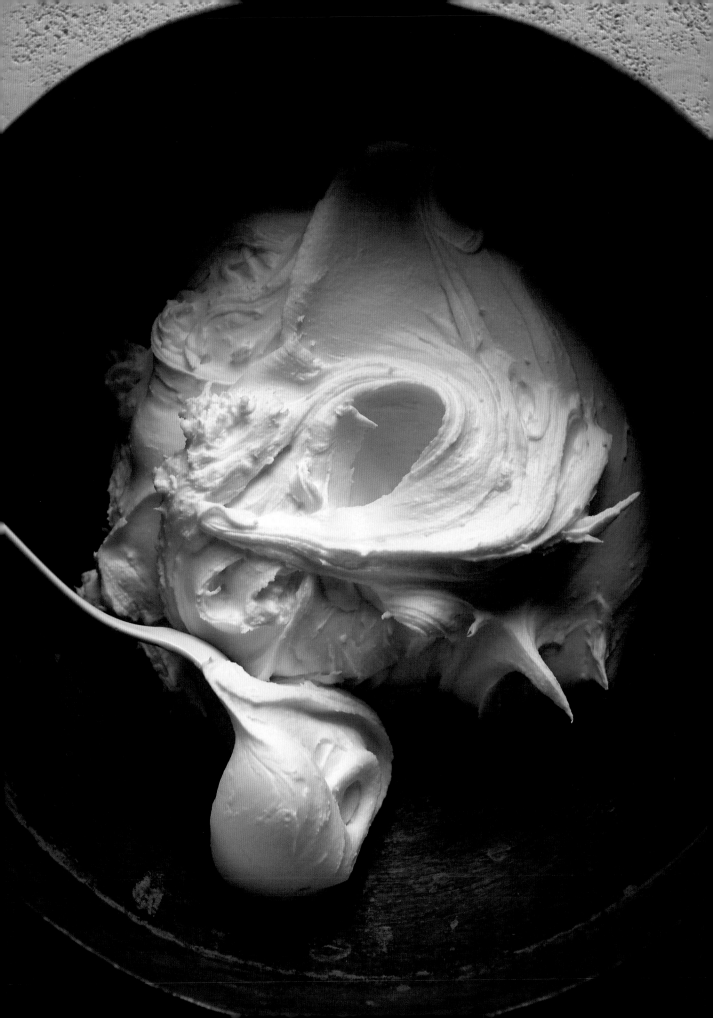

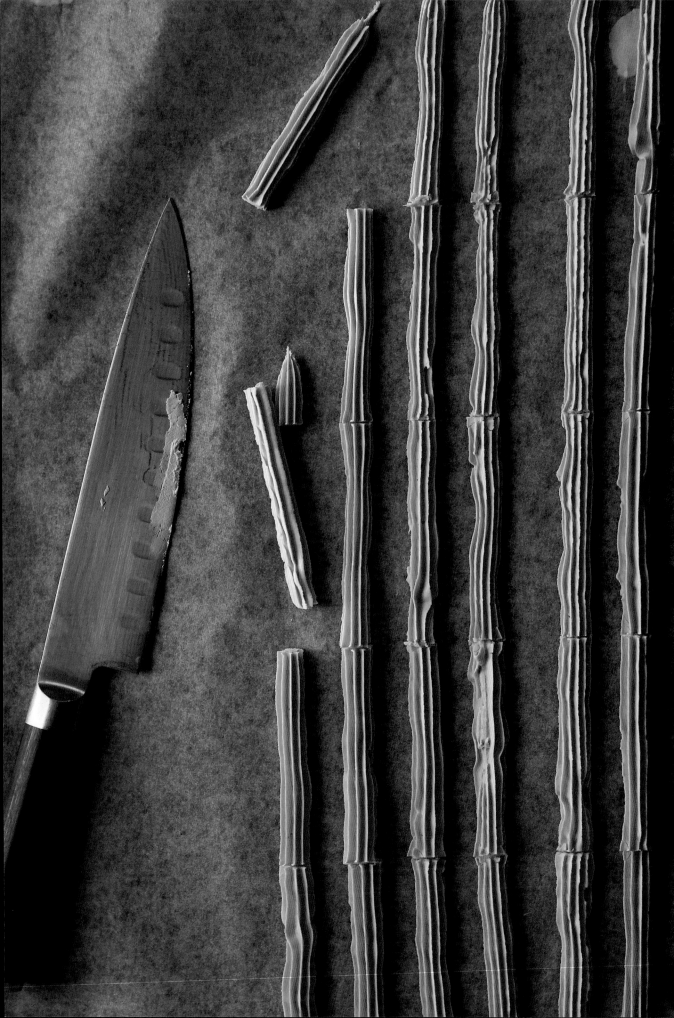

Serves 4

6 gelatine leaves (gold strength)
2 tablespoons liquid glucose
5 cups (800 g) pure icing
   sugar, sifted
1 teaspoon musk flavouring
6 drops of mastic oil
3 drops of red food colouring

Mastic musk sticks

The inspiration for these lies squarely in the great Aussie milk bar. My dad owned a milk bar in Caulfield in the 1980s and he sold the original musk sticks in white paper bags, along with all the other 'mixed lollies' of the time. This is my interpretation using mastic oil as a flavouring. If you can't get hold of mastic oil, use a pinch of crushed mastic beads instead.

Put the gelatine, glucose and 100 ml cold water in the bowl of an electric mixer and place over a saucepan of barely simmering water (make sure the base of the bowl doesn't touch the water). Stir until the gelatine has dissolved, then return the bowl to the mixer and whisk until the mixture resembles marshmallow.

Add the icing sugar all at once and mix, using the paddle attachment, until the sugar has dissolved. Add the remaining ingredients and mix until combined.

Transfer the mixture to a piping bag with a 1 cm star nozzle and pipe onto a baking tray lined with baking paper. Cut into 9 cm long sticks and leave to dry and set at room temperature overnight. Store in an airtight container for up to 1 month.

Acropolis now (see page 240)

Flourless chocolate cake
100 g dark chocolate
   (70% cocoa solids),
   roughly chopped
15 g milk chocolate,
   roughly chopped
50 g unsalted butter
3 egg whites
30 g caster sugar
6 egg yolks

Strawberry mousse
100 g caster sugar
2 egg whites
2 gelatine leaves (gold strength)
150 g strawberries, pureed
   and strained
150 g whipped cream

**Chocolate, coffee and
   mastic soil**
15 g unsalted butter
30 g caster sugar
25 g ground almonds
20 g rice flour
10 g cocoa powder
½ shot of espresso
   (about 1 teaspoon)
salt flakes and mastic oil,
   to taste

Acropolis now

Pictured page 239

We serve hundreds of these at Gazi. A nostalgic reference to the architecture of Athens, much of the appeal is visual, yes, but flavour and texture are what it's all about. At the restaurant we finish the dessert with a cocoa butter spray (as in the photo), but I wouldn't recommend you do this at home – it can get pretty messy! It still looks and tastes amazing without it.

To make the chocolate cake, preheat the oven to 170°C (fan-forced). Grease a 32 cm × 22 cm × 1.5 cm deep baking tray and line with baking paper. Place the chocolate and butter in a heatproof bowl set over a bowl of barely simmering water (don't let the bottom of the bowl touch the water) until melted. Set aside to cool for 2–3 minutes, then stir until smooth. Set aside to cool completely.

Place the egg whites and sugar in the bowl of an electric mixer and whisk until firm peaks form. Gradually add the egg yolks one at a time and whisk until smooth and combined. Fold into the cooled chocolate mixture. Spread the batter over the prepared tray and bake for 8–10 minutes or until just cooked through. Remove from the oven and cool briefly, then place in the freezer to cool completely. Remove from tray, trim the edges and cut into six 8 cm squares.

Meanwhile, to make the strawberry mousse, combine 50 g sugar and 2 teaspoons water in a very clean small saucepan over medium–high heat. Gently swirl the mixture in the pan to agitate until dissolved. Do not stir as this may cause the sugar to crystallise. Increase the heat to high and cook for 3–5 minutes, bringing the syrup up to a temperature of 121°C (check this with a sugar thermometer if possible). If you don't have a sugar thermomenter, keep an eye on the syrup: just as it is about to catch and colour around the saucepan it will be at the correct temperature.

Place the egg whites and remaining sugar in an electric mixer fitted with the whisk attachment and whisk to soft peaks. With the mixer at medium speed, slowly pour the syrup into the bowl of the mixer. Increase to full speed and whisk until the mixture cools completely.

Place the gelatine leaves in a small bowl of water and leave to soften for 1–2 minutes. Heat half the strawberry puree in a small saucepan until just boiling, then remove from the heat. Squeeze the excess water from the softened gelatine and stir into the hot puree until dissolved. Add this to the remaining strawberry puree and stand until cool.

Mix the whipped cream into the Italian meringue, then fold in the strawberry puree.

Lightly grease six ½ cup (125 ml) silicone cupcake moulds. Spoon the strawberry mousse into the moulds and using a palette knife smooth the tops. Place a square of chocolate cake on top and place into the freezer for 2 hours or until set firm.

Carefully sit the moulds in boiling water for 10 seconds ensuring that the water only comes about two-thirds of the way up the side. Invert the moulds and gently push the mousses out onto a tray. If desired, using a fluted scone cutter slightly smaller than the diameter of your mousses, cut the mousses as you would a scone, being careful to only cut the mousse and not the cake. Ease away any excess and release the cutter. This should give a greater impression of a pillar. Return to the fridge until required.

To make the soil, melt the butter in a small frying pan until it starts to brown and takes on a nutty aroma. Remove from the heat and allow to cool. Mix together the sugar, almonds, rice flour and cocoa powder with a fork to remove any lumps, then add the brown butter and begin mixing by hand. Gradually mix in the espresso until the desired consistency is reached – it should now resemble soil. Add salt and mastic oil to taste.

To serve, scatter a few spoonfuls of soil over each serving plate. Top with the mousses and serve.

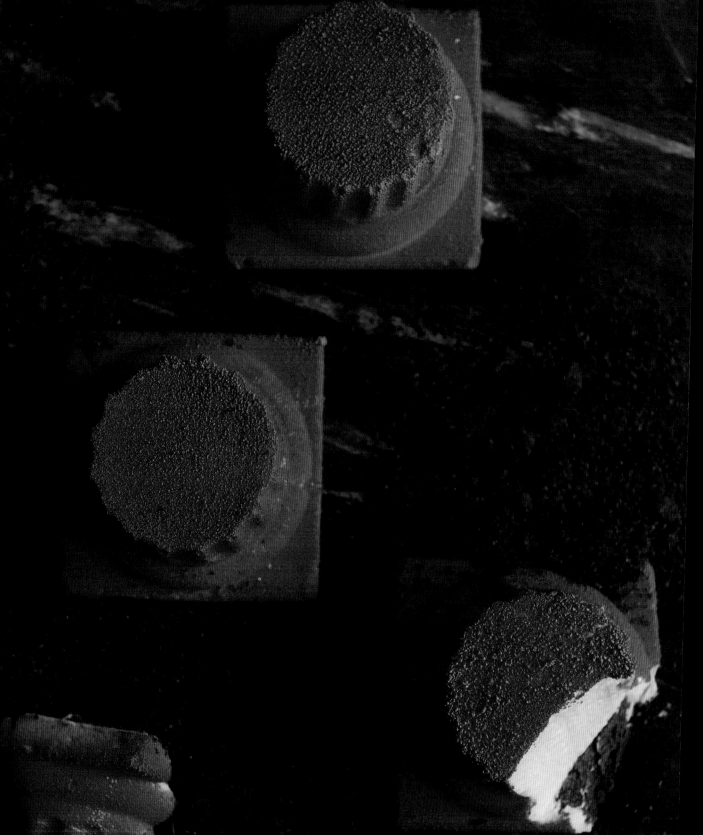

Ouzo-compressed watermelon,
cinnamon yoghurt,
almonds, mint (see page 244)

⅓ watermelon, skin removed,
    cut into 2 cm thick slices
¼ cup (60 ml) ouzo
⅓ cup (95 g) natural
    Greek-style yoghurt
1–2 teaspoons honey, to taste
good pinch of ground cinnamon
2 tablespoons flaked
    almonds, toasted
mint leaves, to garnish

Ouzo-compressed watermelon, cinnamon yoghurt, almonds, mint

Pictured page 243

This is a summer dish to be enjoyed on hot afternoon. As my mother always says, a sweet tooth is there to be nourished at any time of the day. To be at its most refreshing, make sure the watermelon is eaten straight from the fridge. You can still make this if you don't have a cryovac machine – just use a ziplock bag instead.

Place the watermelon and ouzo in a cryovac bag. Seal the bag on high pressure to remove all the air and compress the watermelon. Alternatively, place the watermelon and ouzo in a ziplock bag, press gently to remove all the air and seal. Leave in the fridge overnight.

Mix together the yoghurt, honey and cinnamon.

Remove the watermelon from the bag and arrange on a plate with the yoghurt. Scatter with flaked almonds and mint leaves and serve.

Serves 8

1½ cups (375 ml)
 thickened cream
1 vanilla bean, split,
 seeds scraped
½ cup (40 g) flaked
 almonds, toasted

Meringue
240 g caster sugar
4 egg whites
1 teaspoon rosewater

Orange blossom jelly
200 ml orange blossom water
100 g caster sugar
5 gelatine leaves (gold strength)

Strawberry sauce
250 g strawberries, washed
 and hulled
½ cup (110 g) caster sugar
1½ tablespoons ouzo

Hellenic mess

Pictured page 247

This dish pays homage to
the financial situation in
Greece. We all know it's
a mess. In saying that, there
are two things that no one can
take away from the Greeks:
their pride and their passion.
I say this to young cooks all
the time: if you don't have
pride and passion then don't
become a chef.

To make the meringue, preheat the oven to 200°C (fan-forced) and line
a large baking tray with baking paper. Spread the sugar evenly over the
prepared tray and place in the oven for 8 minutes or until the sugar starts
to dissolve around the edges. When the sugar is nearly ready, start to
whisk the egg whites in an electric mixer until the whites begin to froth.
Carefully add the hot sugar and the rosewater and whisk for a further
10 minutes.

Reduce the oven temperature to 100°C (fan-forced) and line a baking
tray with baking paper. Spread the meringue over the prepared tray,
then transfer to the oven and bake for 3 hours. Remove and allow to
cool completely, then break into bite-sized chunks.

Meanwhile, to make the jelly, place all the ingredients and 200 ml water
in a small saucepan and allow to sit for 2 minutes so the gelatine leaves
soften. Stir over medium heat until the sugar and gelatine have dissolved,
then pour into a suitable container and place in the fridge to set. This will
take at least 2–3 hours.

For the strawberry sauce, blitz the strawberries in a food processor,
then pass through a fine-mesh sieve. Place in a saucepan with the sugar
and ouzo stir over medium heat until the sugar has dissolved. Store in
the fridge until needed.

Shortly before you are ready to serve, whip the cream and vanilla
seeds until firm peaks form.

Layer the chunks of meringue, jelly and dollops of whipped cream in
a serving dish. At the last minute, drizzle over the strawberry sauce
and finish with a sprinkling of flaked almonds.

Hellenic mess
(See page 245)

Makes about 14

200 g clarified butter
(see note below)
500 g unsalted cashews
14 sheets filo pastry
(see page 299), each sheet
about 20 cm × 15 cm
1 kg caster sugar

finely grated zest and
juice of 1 lemon
10 cardamom pods,
lightly crushed
½ cup (75 g) sesame seeds,
lightly toasted

Baklava 1.0
Cashew and cardamom escargot

Who invented baklava? The Persians? Turks? Greeks? Personally, I think it was the Persians, but at the end of the day who cares? Baklava is perfection on a plate, with every mouthful somehow managing to be sweet, chewy and crunchy all at the same time. Just watch the cardamom – if you add too much, this beautiful fragrant spice can become soapy and overpowering.

Note:
To clarify butter, place the desired quantity of butter in a saucepan and place over low heat until it has melted. Gently simmer until the foam rises to the top. Keep skimming the top until the foam seems to stop rising. Strain through a coffee filter or muslin cloth before using. Store in the fridge until needed.

Preheat the oven to 170°C (fan-forced). Lightly brush a baking tray (about 33 cm × 23 cm) with clarified butter.

Place the cashews in a food processor and pulse until finely chopped (take care not to overprocess otherwise it will become a paste).

Lay a sheet of filo pastry on a clean bench with the shorter edge closest to you and lightly brush with clarified butter. Place a dowel rod on the sheet, approximately 2 cm from the bottom edge. Sprinkle a small handful of ground nuts across the dowel. Fold the bottom edge over the dowel, then keep rolling until you reach the top edge.

Push both ends of the pastry in towards the centre so that the pastry crinkles and the dowel pokes out the ends. Slide out the dowel and roll up like a snail or 'escargot', then place the pastry on one end of the prepared tray. Repeat until you have about 14 pieces, arranging them snugly on the tray. Brush the tops with clarified butter, then bake for 25–30 minutes or until golden.

Meanwhile, combine the sugar, lemon zest and juice, cardamom and 450 ml water in a saucepan and bring to the boil, stirring until the sugar has dissolved. Reduce the heat and simmer for 2 minutes, then set aside to cool to room temperature.

Remove the pastries from the oven and cool for 5 minutes, then strain the syrup evenly over the top. Sprinkle with sesame seeds and cool to room temperature before serving.

Loukoumi and
pistachio baklava
(see page 254)

Makes about 16 pieces

200 g clarified butter
  (see note, page 251)
500 g shelled, roasted pistachios
16 sheets filo pastry
  (see page 299), each sheet
  about 20 cm × 15 cm

200 g honey
200 g caster sugar
2 teaspoons rosewater
4 pieces rose loukoumi
  (Turkish delight)

Baklava 2.0
Loukoumi and
pistachio baklava

Pictured
Page 253

This is a great variation on traditional baklava. The Turkish delight (loukoumi) adds a chewy texture that I find really hard to resist. Just take care when buying your Turkish delight – make sure it's not too sickly sweet or it will flatten the flavour of the other ingredients. Baklava should always be served at room temperature.

Preheat the oven to 170°C (fan-forced). Lightly brush two baking trays with clarified butter.

Place the pistachios in a food processor and pulse until finely chopped (take care not to overprocess otherwise it will become a paste).

Lay a sheet of filo pastry on a clean bench with the shorter edge closest to you and lightly brush with clarified butter. Place a dowel rod on the sheet, approximately 2 cm from the bottom edge. Sprinkle a small handful of nuts across the dowel. Fold the bottom edge over the dowel, then keep rolling until you reach the top edge. Push the filo together and remove from the dowel. Place on one of the prepared trays. Repeat to make about 16 pieces, reserving a handful of pistachios to garnish. Brush the tops with clarified butter and bake for 30 minutes or until golden.

Meanwhile, combine the honey, sugar, rosewater and 450 ml water in a saucepan and bring to the boil, stirring until the sugar has dissolved. Reduce the heat and simmer for 2 minutes, then set aside to cool to room temperature.

Remove the baklava from the oven and cool for 5 minutes, then pour the syrup evenly over the pastries. Cut the loukoumi into small pieces with kitchen scissors and place on top of the baklava. Sprinkle over the reserved pistachios and cool to room temperature before serving.

Makes about 70 small pieces

1 kg slivered almonds
½ cup (80 g) fine semolina
pinch of salt flakes
1 vanilla bean, split,
   seeds scraped
500 g clarified butter
   (see note, page 251)
40 sheets filo pastry
   (see page 299), each sheet
   about 33 cm × 23 cm

about 70 cloves
750 g caster sugar
250 g honey
finely grated zest and juice
   of 1 orange

Pictured page 257

Baklava 3.0
Spiced almond and vanilla baklava

What I love about baklava is that the recipe changes all the time, depending on who's making it and where they come come from. It's a great way for cooks to put their personal stamp on it. This combination of almond and vanilla is beautiful, and adding just a pinch of salt brings out the flavour of the almonds. Make sure the syrup has cooled completely before pouring it over the hot pastries (or do it the other way: hot syrup and cold pastries – just make sure one is hot and one is cold).

Place the almonds, semolina, salt and vanilla seeds (reserve the pod for the syrup) in a food processor and pulse until finely chopped (take care not to overprocess otherwise it will become a paste).

Lightly brush a baking dish (about 33 cm × 23 cm) with clarified butter. Place a sheet of filo in the prepared dish, folding any overhanging pastry into the tray, and brush with clarified butter. Layer and butter another six sheets of pastry, then sprinkle a good handful of the almond mixture evenly over the top. Lay another sheet of filo on top, brush with butter and top with another handful of almonds. Repeat this layering until you have used all the almond mixture. Press down gently on the baklava to compress the nuts. Top with a sheet of filo and brush with butter, then layer and butter another six sheets of pastry. Press again firmly to compress the layers and thoroughly brush the top with butter. Transfer to the fridge for 1 hour to set.

Preheat the oven to 170°C (fan-forced).

Score the baklava lengthways into five strips about 4.5 cm wide (you should only cut through the top layers of pastry), then cut widthways into seven strips. Cut across each square piece to form a triangle, and stud each one with a clove. Bake for 40 minutes or until golden.

Meanwhile, combine the sugar, honey, orange zest and juice, reserved vanilla pod and 450 ml water in a saucepan and bring to the boil, stirring until the sugar has dissolved. Reduce the heat and simmer for 2 minutes, then set aside to cool to room temperature.

Remove the baklava from the oven and cool for 5 minutes, then strain the syrup evenly over the top. Allow the baklava to cool completely (this will take a good few hours), then cut into pieces following the scored lines.

Spiced almond and vanilla baklava
(see page 255)

Makes 1

at least 1 heaped tablespoon
   instant coffee granules
20 ml sugar syrup
   (see note below)
½ cup (125 ml) full-cream milk
ice cubes

Frappe 'Glyfada Style'

This is a Greek foam-covered version of iced coffee made from instant coffee. Everyone has their own preferences when it comes to making a frappe, so the quantities given are just a guide. Pick your ingredients and decide how much you want to add, and enjoy.

Place the coffee granules, sugar syrup, milk and 30–60 ml cold water in a milkshake maker or blender and blend for about 30 seconds. Pour into a glass or cup filled with ice.

Sugar syrup
The easiest way to make a sugar syrup is following a method called 50/50 (that is, the same quantity of each). For example, combine 500 ml boiling water and 500 g caster sugar in a large saucepan and stir over medium heat until the sugar has dissolved and the liquid is clear. Leave to cool, then store in the fridge until needed.

Makes 1

sugar, to taste (optional)
1 heaped teaspoon Greek coffee

Greek coffee

I pride myself on making a great cup of Greek coffee. This is a strong brew, served with foam on top and the grounds in the bottom of the cup. You will need a briki (Greek coffee pot) and a demitasse (small) cup to make it properly.

Place 1 cup (125 ml) cold water in a briki and add sugar to taste, if desired. Add the coffee, then place over medium–low heat and stir until it has dissolved. **Then don't stir it again.** Let the coffee heat slowly; as it does, foam will start to rise in the briki before it boils.

Once the foam rises to the top, remove the briki from the heat. Spoon the foam into the cup, then pour in the coffee, taking care not to disturb the foam.

Makes 1

30 ml kahlua
30 ml amaretto
1 shot of fresh espresso
pinch of salt flakes

Honeycomb
75 g honey
140 ml liquid glucose
400 g caster sugar
1 tablespoon bicarbonate of soda

Gazi
espressotini

This is my adaption of the espressotini cocktail made famous by British bartender Dick Bradsell. Any leftover honeycomb should be stored in an airtight container in the freezer, where it will keep for a few months. Halve the quantities if you like.

To make the honeycomb, place the honey, glucose, sugar and ½ cup (125 ml) water in a deep saucepan. Bring to the boil, then immediately reduce to a simmer. Continue to simmer for about 10 minutes or until the edges of the syrup become light golden – the honeycomb will continue to darken so don't worry if it seems pale when you add the bicarb. Add the bicarbonate of soda and whisk for 5 seconds, then immediately pour the honeycomb onto a silicon mat or a tray lined with baking paper. Allow to cool completely, then break the honeycomb into pieces and store in an airtight container until needed.

Place the kahlua, amaretto, espresso and salt in a cocktail shaker and shake vigorously to combine. Strain into a chilled ouzo glass (or any short glass) and garnish with a sprinkling of honeycomb crumbs.

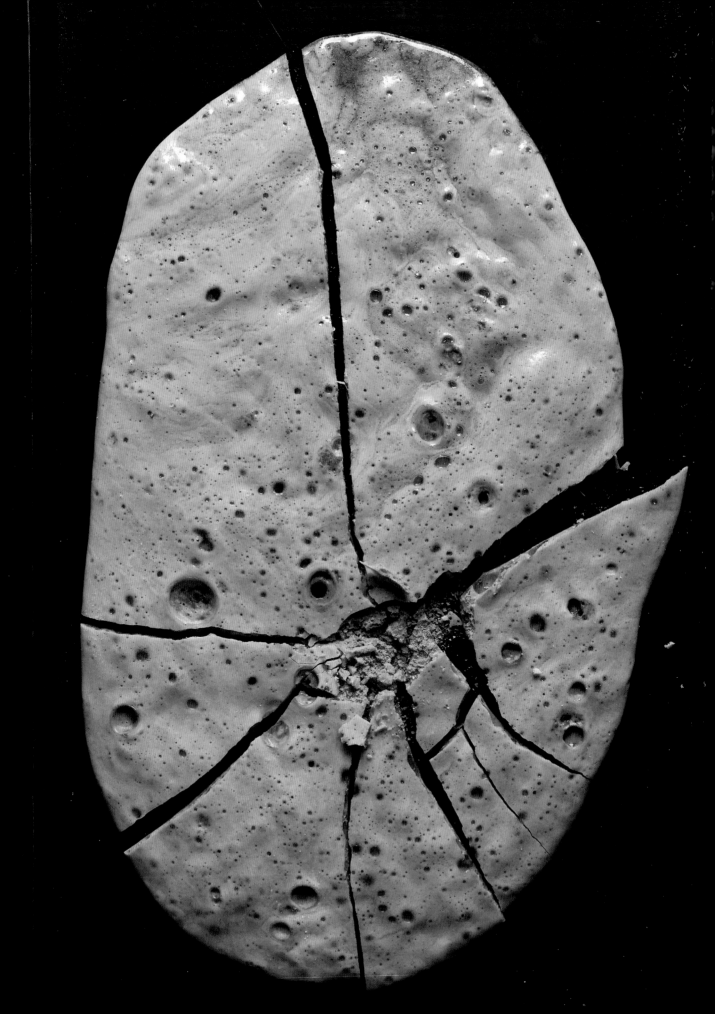

Makes 1

ice cubes
20 ml lemon juice
330 ml soda water
   (or sparkling water)
1 scoop of vanilla ice-cream
   (see page 302)

Visinada
1 kg pitted cherries
500 g caster sugar
6 star anise
small handful of cloves
1 cinnamon stick

Sour cherry spider

Everybody loves a spider!
Here I give this childhood
favourite a makeover with
some classic Greek flavours.
Visinada is a well-known
Greek drink made with
sour cherry cordial and cold
water – once made, it will
keep in the fridge for a few
months.

To make the visinada, bring 1 cup (250 ml) water to the boil in a deep
saucepan. Add half the cherries, then reduce the heat and simmer for
5 minutes. Add the sugar and blend with a stick blender until it has
dissolved. Stir in the spices and simmer for a further 15 minutes, then
strain, discarding the solids. Allow to cool, then add the remaining
cherries and refrigerate until needed.

Fill a chilled highball or spider glass with ice. Pour the lemon juice,
soda water and 30 ml visinada into the glass, add two or three cherries
and finish with a scoop of ice-cream.

Mountain tea 'Hot Toddy'

(See page 274)

Makes 1

30 ml Greek brandy
    (or any type of brandy)
20 ml lemon juice
1 cinnamon stick
1 star anise

Mountain tea honey water
500 g honey
2 large handfuls of Greek
    mountain tea leaves
small handful of chamomile
    tea leaves
6 cloves
4 star anise
small handful of coriander seeds

Mountain tea 'Hot Toddy'

Pictured page 273

This deliciously warming drink is made with a moreish combination of Greek brandy, honey, lemon juice and spices – just the thing to fight off the winter chills. The best place to source Greek mountain tea is online, as there are many suppliers to choose from.

To make the mountain tea honey water, bring 2 cups (500 ml) water to the boil in a deep saucepan. Add the remaining ingredients and simmer for 15 minutes, then strain, discarding the solids. Allow to cool, then refrigerate until needed.

Combine the brandy, lemon juice and 30 ml mountain tea honey water in a saucepan over medium heat and add enough hot water to suit your taste. Bring it to just below the boil, then pour into a Toddy glass or a large coffee cup or mug. Garnish with a cinnamon stick and a star anise and serve.

Makes 1

60 ml Greek brandy
   (or any type of brandy)
30 ml grapefruit juice
dash of Angostura Bitters
ice cubes
crushed pistachios, to garnish

Baklava syrup
250 ml sugar syrup (see page 262)
250 g honey
250 g shelled roasted pistachios
pinch of salt flakes

Baklava Cocktail

Pictured page 277

Anyone who knows me knows how much I love baklava, so it was inevitable that one day I would turn it into a cocktail. With a definite leaning towards the sweeter side of the palate, this drink is designed to be an after-dinner indulgence. Leftover syrup will keep in the fridge for a few months, but I bet it won't last that long – try serving it with ice-cream!

To make the baklava syrup, place all the ingredients in a saucepan and warm over low heat, stirring. Remove from the heat and blend with a stick blender until smooth and creamy. Strain and leave to cool, then refrigerate until needed.

Place the brandy, grapefruit juice, bitters and 20 ml baklava syrup in a cocktail shaker and fill up with ice. Give it a good shake, then double-strain into a chilled cocktail glass and garnish with crushed pistachios.

Baklava Cocktail
(See page 275)

Makes 1

3 thin slices cucumber
3 cherry tomatoes
5 mint leaves
crushed ice
30 ml Pimms
20 ml gin
10 ml ouzo
1 × 300 ml bottle tonic water
1 cube of feta
1 sprig mint, extra

Horiatiki tonic

Just as every Greek village has its own Greek 'Horiatiki' salad, I have created my own unique G&T. Made with classic Greek salad ingredients and a touch of aromatic Pimms, this light, fresh-tasting drink is particularly good as an aperitif before your meal or any time you need a refreshing cocktail during the warmer months.

Lightly muddle one slice of cucumber and two cherry tomatoes in a highball glass (taking care not to bruise them). Add the mint leaves, remaining cucumber and a handful of crushed ice. Pour in the Pimms, gin and ouzo, then top with tonic water.

Skewer the feta and remaining tomato on a long toothpick and use as a garnish, along with a sprig of mint.

Makes about 1.5 litres

1 kg ripe truss tomatoes
small handful of basil leaves
2–3 teaspoons salt flakes
3 teaspoons caster sugar
Tabasco sauce, to taste

Tomato tea

This isn't really a tea; it's the idea of a clear tea using the heady flavour and fragrance of tomatoes. The secret to success here has nothing to do with the recipe; everything hinges on the ripeness of the tomatoes. ONLY make this when tomatoes are in season and ripened on the vine. Otherwise, forget about it.

Place the tomatoes, basil, salt and sugar in a blender and blend until finely chopped but not a puree. Take care not to blend for too long otherwise it will be difficult to extract enough liquid.

Taste the mixture and add Tabasco to taste – a few splashes should do it, depending on the ripeness of the tomatoes.

Pour into a sieve lined with muslin set over a bowl or container and leave refrigerated overnight. The next day, lightly squeeze the remaining juice through the sieve.

Discard the pulp in the sieve and serve the tea chilled. Store in the fridge for up to a week.

Makes 1

2 Lebanese cucumbers
30 ml ouzo, or to taste

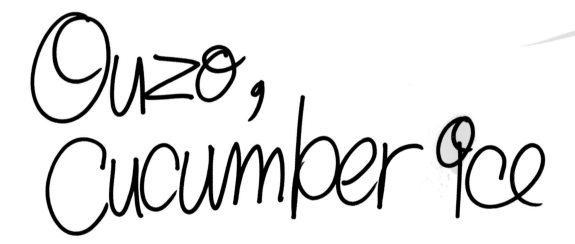

This simple drink is a new take on traditional ouzo and ice. At The Press Club we use cucumber ice to complement the herbal aniseed flavours of ouzo. Never one to do things by halves, I also like to make the ice in the shape of small cucumbers, but you don't have to go to those lengths! The magic is all in the flavour.

Remove the skin from the cucumber and blend the flesh. Pour the cucumber liquid into an ice-cube tray and freeze until needed.

Pour the ouzo into an ouzo glass (or any short glass) and add cucumber ice cubes, to taste. Enjoy!

village bread (see page 288)

Makes 1 loaf

1 × 7 g sachet dried yeast
⅔ cup (100 g) plain
    wholemeal flour
2⅔ cups (400 g) type '00' flour,
    plus extra for dusting
2 teaspoons salt flakes
2 tablespoons natural
    Greek-style yoghurt
2 tablespoons extra virgin
    olive oil
2 tablespoons honey

Village bread

Pictured
Page 287

Dissolve the yeast in 70 ml warm water. Stir in 2 tablespoons of the wholemeal flour until there are no lumps, then cover with plastic film and set aside for 30 minutes.

Place the remaining flours in a large bowl and make a well in the centre. Add 1½ cups (375 ml) warm water and the remaining ingredients, including the yeast starter, and mix with your hands until the dough starts to come together. Turn out onto a floured surface and knead until smooth. Transfer the dough to a lightly oiled bowl, cover with plastic film and leave to prove for 1½ hours.

Place the dough on a floured surface and knead again for several minutes. Shape the dough into a rectangle, then place on a lightly floured tray and dust the top with flour. Cover with a dry tea towel and then a damp tea towel, and leave to prove in a warm place for 1¼ hours.

Position a rack in the lower third of your oven and preheat the oven to 250°C (fan-forced). For best results, preheat the oven for about 30 minutes with an upside-down baking tray or a pizza stone on the prepared rack to create more thermal mass.

Once the bread has proved, slice some diagonal cuts in the top. Carefully place the bread on the hot tray or stone and spray with a little water. (This will add steam, slowing down the formation of a crust, giving the bread more volume.)

Bake for 15 minutes, then reduce the temperature to 200°C (fan-forced) and bake for a further 30 minutes. Turn the oven off and crack open the oven door with the handle of a wooden spoon, then cook for 10 minutes more.

Remove the bread from the oven and tap the bottom – it should sound hollow. Cool completely on a wire rack before slicing.

Makes 8 small pita breads

1 tablespoon salt flakes
3 teaspoons dried yeast
2 tablespoons extra virgin
   olive oil
1 tablespoon natural
   Greek-style yoghurt
1 tablespoon honey
4 cups (600 g) type '00' flour,
   plus extra if needed
semolina, for dusting
olive oil spray

Pictured page 291

Place the salt, yeast, olive oil, yoghurt, honey, 2 cups (300 g) flour and 300 ml warm water in the bowl of an electric mixer and beat until smooth. Cover with plastic film and prove in the fridge for at least 12 hours, preferably overnight.

The next day, add the remaining flour to the mixture. Fit the electric mixer with a dough hook and beat on a low speed until the flour is fully incorporated. Increase the speed to medium and beat for 2–3 minutes or until the dough comes away from the bowl and is tacky but not sticky when touched. Add a little more flour if needed to reach the desired consistency.

Turn out the dough onto a lightly floured benchtop and knead for 1 minute or until smooth. Divide the dough into eight even-sized pieces and knead into balls. (If you are making large pita breads, divide the dough into four portions.)

Dust the benchtop with semolina and, using a semolina-dusted rolling pin, roll out the balls until they're about 5 mm thick, sprinkling with extra semolina to prevent sticking, if needed. Prick all over with a fork, then place on semolina-dusted baking trays and leave in a warm, dry spot to prove for 30 minutes.

Preheat a non-stick frying pan over medium heat until hot (or a chargrill pan or barbecue grill or flatplate). Lightly spray the pan with oil, then add the breads one at a time and cook for 2 minutes on each side. Serve immediately or reheat again later in the pan.

Pita bread
(See page 289)

Makes about 1½ cups (450 g)

1 small clove garlic
3 egg yolks
1 teaspoon Dijon mustard
1 teaspoon salt flakes
2 tablespoons lemon juice
1 tablespoon white wine vinegar
400 ml vegetable oil

Mayonnaise

Preheat the oven to 180°C (fan-forced). Wrap the garlic clove in foil and roast for 10–15 minutes or until soft. Allow to cool, then remove the skin.

Place the garlic, egg yolks, mustard, salt, lemon juice and vinegar in a bowl and blend with a stick blender. Slowly add the vegetable oil, drop by drop at first then in a slow, steady stream, until the mixture is thick and creamy. Store in a jar in the fridge for up to 1 week.

Makes 150–200 g

1 litre full-cream milk
1 teaspoon salt flakes
⅓ cup (80 ml) white vinegar

Pictured
Page 294

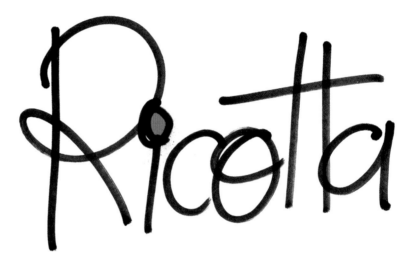

Place the milk and salt in a medium saucepan over high eat and bring
to a simmer. Remove from the heat.

Combine the vinegar and ¾ cup (185 ml) water in a jug. Pour into the milk
and stir gently for a few seconds – you will instantly see curds start to
form. Be careful not to over-stir as this may cause the curds to toughen.

Place the saucepan in a sink of cold water and leave to sit for about
20 minutes.

Line a colander with a clean J-cloth or a square of muslin. Using a slotted
spoon, gently lift the curds out of the whey and place in the colander.

Bring the remaining contents of the saucepan (the whey) back to the
boil and repeat steps 3 and 4 to capture any remaining curds.

Tie up the edges of the cloth and sit the colander over a larger bowl
to catch any excess liquid. Refrigerate for at least 2 hours before using.
Ricotta will keep in an airtight container in the fridge for up to 4 days.

Ricotta (see page 293)

Makes about 1.25 kg

1 litre full-fat milk
1 cup (280 g) thick yoghurt
   (must contain 'live active
   yoghurt cultures')
1 tablespoon honey
1 teaspoon salt flakes

House-made yoghurt

Preheat the oven to 130°C (fan-forced).

Wash five or six 1 cup (250 ml) or two 600 ml glass jars and lids
in warm soapy water and rinse well in clean hot water. Do not dry.
Arrange in a shallow baking tray right side up and place in the oven
for 5 minutes to sterilise.

Meanwhile, pour the milk into a medium saucepan over medium heat
and bring to a simmer. Remove from the heat and allow to drop in
temperature to 40°C. Whisk in the yoghurt, honey and salt.

Place a small fine-mesh sieve over the opening of each jar and pour in
the mixture, leaving a 2–3 cm gap at the top. Seal with the lids and keep
in a warm place (around 30°C) for 12 hours. Transfer to the fridge and
refrigerate for 3 hours or until set. The yoghurt will keep for up to 2 weeks
in sealed jars and 4–6 days once opened.

Makes about 1.5 litres

3 kg chicken carcasses
5 white onions, roughly chopped
½ bunch celery, trimmed, washed
  and roughly chopped
1 kg carrots, trimmed, washed
  and roughly chopped
2 leeks, white part only, washed
  and roughly chopped
3 bay leaves
10 white peppercorns

Chicken Stock

Using a cleaver, cut the chicken carcasses into four equal pieces. Place them in a colander and wash under running water, then drain and transfer to a large stockpot. Cover with cold water and bring to the boil, skimming the froth off the surface with a ladle. Reduce to a simmer and add the remaining ingredients.

Simmer for 2 hours, skimming frequently, then strain through a muslin-lined sieve, discarding the solids.

Return the stock to a clean saucepan and simmer over medium heat until the liquid has reduced by two-thirds (this will concentrate the flavour). Pour into small containers and store in the freezer for up to 2 months, or in the fridge for up to 7 days.

Makes 500 g

2⅔ cups (400 g) plain flour
1 teaspoon salt flakes
2 tablespoons extra virgin olive oil
cornflour, for dusting

Filo pastry

Pictured
Page 301

Place the flour, salt, olive oil and 200 ml warm water in a food processor
and blend for 1–2 minutes or until the dough comes together in a ball.

Place the dough on a clean surface and knead until smooth. Transfer to
a lightly greased bowl, cover with plastic film and rest in a warm place
for about 2 hours.

Divide the dough into eight pieces, then roll out each piece to a thickness
of about 1 cm, dusting with cornflour to prevent sticking. Cover with
a clean tea towel and rest for 10 minutes.

Working with one piece of dough at a time, roll out the sheets using
a pasta machine, starting at the largest setting and working to the thinnest
setting. Cut the filo into your desired shape and use immediately. Cover
any unused portions with a tea towel to prevent them from drying out.
Leftovers may also be wrapped in plastic film and frozen.

filo pastry (see page 299)

Serves 4

2 cups (500 ml) thickened cream
2 cups (500 ml) full-cream milk
1 vanilla bean, split, seeds scraped
5 egg yolks
200 g caster sugar

Vanilla Ice-Cream

Place the cream, milk and vanilla seeds in a large heavy-based saucepan and gently bring to a simmer.

Meanwhile, whisk the egg yolks and sugar in a large heaproof bowl until the mixture becomes pale yellow. Slowly pour the cream mixture over the eggs, whisking constantly, then return the mixture to the pan and stir with a spatula over low heat until it reaches 80°C on a sugar thermometer.

Strain the custard through a fine-mesh sieve into a clean heatproof bowl, then sit in a larger bowl half-filled with ice and stir to cool down rapidly and stop the cooking process. When completely cold, transfer to an ice-cream machine and churn according to the manufacturer's instructions. Store in the freezer. Homemade ice-cream is best eaten within 3 days.

Efkharisto

Natalie, James and Michaela: the three of you put it all into perspective. You make everything worthwhile. Words cannot express the love I have for the three of you.

Mum, thank you for your food love and the great recipes in this book. Dad, thank you for giving me a love of working hard – and soccer. My sister and brother, the three of us are so different, but at the end of the day one thing is for sure: I love you both. My nieces, nephews and godchildren: I love your guts!

Lauren, thank you for your commitment to me.
Loyal – that's what you are.

To my business partners Uncle Joe, Tony (aka FBT), George (aka Siko) and Travis (aka Bipa): thank you for understanding my dream and believing in it.

I employ over 300 staff in my group: the chefs, waitstaff, bartenders, kitchen hands, glass polishers, cleaners, reservations team, accounts department. Every single one of you plays a part in this massive jigsaw puzzle that I love and adore.

My management team:
Nick, Fleur, Ryan, Valeria, Loris, Nikki, Rob, Kelly, Chris, Chrysa, Kieran, Kerryn, Luke, Rob, Guillaume, Simon, Alex, Denis, Arron, Anthony.

All my suppliers, producers and growers who make my life easy. Without you we chefs are nothing.

Matt, Gary and all my MasterChef family, thank you for the laughs and the memories.

To the team that gives me a platform, a space to create and for my diners to enjoy. Thank you Rodney and the team from March Studios, and CBD for building our venues on time. Thanks for putting up with our craziness.

The Penguin team for their patience with me: sorry, but thank you! Julie, Rachel, Evi and the rest of you rock!

Earl Carter, geez you're good. I loved working with you and I hope you like Greek food now.

To Lee Blaylock, thank you for your amazing eye for detail. Detail is what makes a good thing great.

And Paul Scott and Glen Flood for your recipe testing and lots of laughs.

Index

306

LANTERN

UK | USA | Canada | Ireland | Australia
India | New Zealand | South Africa | China

Penguin Books is part of the Penguin Random House group of companies
whose addresses can be found at global.penguinrandomhouse.com.

Penguin
Random House
Australia

First published by Penguin Group (Australia), 2015
This paperback edition first published by Penguin Australia Pty Ltd, 2017

Design by Evi O. © Penguin Group (Australia)
Photography by Earl Carter
Styling by Lee Blaylock
Typeset in 8.75/11.5 pt Neuzeit S by
Post Pre-press Group, Brisbane, Queensland
Colour separation by Splitting Image Colour Studio, Clayton, Victoria
Printed and bound in China by 1010 Printing International Limited

National Library of Australia
Cataloguing-in-Publication data:

Calombaris, George, author.
Greek / George Calombaris; Earl Carter.
ISBN: 9780143574224 (paperback)
Cooking, Greek.
Cooking.
Carter, Earl, 1957– photographer.

penguin.com.au/lantern

If this is a dream, please don't wake me up.

— GPC